HIP POETRY 2012

Hip Poetry 2012

Editors

Diana May-Waldman
Mitchell Waldman
Joe McEvoy

WIND PUBLICATIONS

Copyright © 2012 by Worldwide Hippies. Printed in the United States of America. All rights reserved. No part of this book may be reproduced in any manner without permission, except for brief quotations embodied in critical articles or reviews. For information, address Wind Publications, 600 Overbrook Drive, Nicholasville, Kentucky 40356.

International Standard Book Number 978-1-936138-43-2
Library of Congress Control Number 2011945541

First edition

Front Cover — Joe McEvoy, wind in his hair.

Contributor Index

Wendy Babiak	171
Lee Balan	124
Jill Battson	151
John Burroughs	208
Dianne Borsenik	214
Cynthia L. Bryant	161
Donald R. Carson, Sr.	204
Michael Castro	62
Jim Christy	166
Susan Deer Cloud	70
Michelle Dawson	225
Geri Digiorno	59
DubbleX	95
Gloria Frym	119
Timothy Gager	20
Bill Harrison	226
Laura Strathman Hulka	24
James Lee Jobe	6
Paul Krassner	1
David LaBounty	179
Angel Caywood Lambert	199
Joy Leftow	79
Skye Leslie	165
Louise Levi	53
Stephen Lewandowski	56
Lyn Lifshin	26
Teck Loh	88
Merrit Malloy	221

Diana May-Waldman	175, 223
Martha Meltzer	52
David Meltzer	55
Michele Close Mills	49
Jesse Mitchell	46
Ars Moriendi	206
Craig Murray	103
William Page	218
Seelan Palay	115
Sherry Pasquarello	75
Andrew J. Pensabene, III	33
Hans Plomp	40
Mikel K. Poet	99
Robert Priest	93
Deena Remiel	17
John Roche	201
David A. Ross	9
Michael Rothenberg	42
Harris Schiff	190
Misty Serna	102
Ernest Stewart	38
Melissa Studdard	155
Mitchell Waldman	126
Viola Weinberg	158
Brandon Wilson	110
David Wiseman	83
Jordan Zinovich	196
Contributors' biographical notes	254

My Acid Trip With Groucho Marx

Paul Krassner

LSD was influencing music, painting, spirituality, and the stock market. Timothy Leary once let me listen in on a call from a Wall Street broker thanking him for turning him onto acid because it gave him the courage to sell short. Leary had a certain sense of pride about the famous folks he and his associates had introduced to the drug.

"But," he told me, "I consider Otto Preminger one of our failures."

I first met Preminger in 1960 while I was conducting a panel on censorship for Playboy. He had defied Hollywood's official seal of approval by refusing to change the script of "The Moon Is Blue." He wouldn't take out the word virgin. At the end of our interview, he asked, "Ven you tronscripe dis, vill you vix op my Henglish?"

"Oh, sure," I replied quickly. "Of course."

"Vy? Vot's drong viz my Henglish?"

I saw Otto Preminger again in 1967. He was making a movie called Skidoo, starring Jackie Gleason as a retired criminal. Preminger told me he had originally intended the role for Frank Sinatra. I was hanging around with friends from the Hog Farm, who were extras in the movie. Skidoo was proacid propaganda thinly disguised as a comedy adventure. However, LSD was not why the FBI was annoyed with the film. Rather, according to Gleason's FBI files, the FBI objected to one scene in the script where a file cabinet is stolen from an FBI building. Gleason was later approved as a special FBI contact in the entertainment business.

One of the characters in Skidoo was a Mafia chieftain named God. Screenwriter Bill Cannon had suggested Groucho Marx for the part. Preminger said it wasn't a good idea, but since they were already shooting and that particular character was needed on the set in three days, Groucho would be playing God after all. I had dinner with Groucho. He was concerned about the script of Skidoo because it pretty much advocated LSD, which he had never tried, but he was curious. Moreover, he felt a certain responsibility to his young audience not to steer them wrong, so could I possibly get him some pure stuff and would I care to accompany him on a trip? I did not play hard to get. We arranged to ingest those little white tablets one afternoon at the home of an actress in Beverly Hills.

Groucho was especially interested in the counterculutral aspects of LSD. I mentioned a couple of incidents that particularly tickled him, and his eyes sparkled with delight. One was about how, on Haight Street, runaway youngsters—refugees from their own families—had stood outside a special tourist bus—guided by a driver "trained in sociological significance" —and held mirrors up to the cameras pointing at them from the windows, so that the tourists would get photos of themselves trying to take photos. The other was about the day that LSD became illegal. In San Francisco, at precisely two o'clock in the afternoon, a cross-fertilization of mass protest and tribal celebration had taken place, as several hundred young people simultaneously swallowed tabs of acid while the police stood by helplessly. "Internal possession wasn't against the law," I explained to Groucho

"And they trusted their friends more than they trusted the government," he said. "I like that."

We had a period of silence and a period of listening to music. I was accustomed to playing rock and roll while tripping, but the record collection at this house consisted entirely of classical music and Broadway show albums. First, we listened to the "Bach Cantata No. 7."

"I'm supposed to be Jewish," Groucho said, "but I was seeing the most beautiful visions of Gothic cathedrals. Do you think Bach knew he was doing that?"

"I don't know. I was seeing beehives and honeycombs myself."

Later, we were listening to the score of a musical comedy, Fanny. There was one song called "Welcome Home," where the lyrics go something like, "Welcome home, says the clock," and the chair says, "Welcome home," and so do various other pieces of furniture. Groucho started acting out each line, as though he were actually being greeted by the clock, the chair, and the rest of the furniture. He was like a child, charmed by his own ability to respond to the music that way.

There was a bowl of fruit on the dining room table. During a snack, he said, "I never thought eating a nice juicy plum would be the biggest thrill of my life."

Then we talked about the sexual revolution. Groucho asked, "Have you ever laid two ladies together?" I told him about the time that I was being interviewed by a couple of students from a Catholic girls' school. Suddenly Sheila Campion, The Realist's Scapegoat, and Marcia Ridge, the Shit-On—she had given herself that title because "What could be lower than a Scapegoat?"—walked out of their office totally nude. "Sorry to interrupt, Paul," said Sheila, "but it's Wednesday—time for our weekly orgy." The interviewers left in a hurry. Sheila and Marcia led me up the stairs to my loft bed, and we had a delicious threesome. It had never happened before and it would never happen again.

At one point in our conversation, Groucho somehow got into a negative space. He was equally cynical about institutions, such as marriage—"legal quicksand"—and individuals, such as Lyndon Johnson—"that potato-head."

Eventually, I asked, "What gives you hope?"

He thought for a moment. Then he just said one word: "People."

He told me about one of his favorite contestants on You Bet Your Life. "He was an elderly gentleman with white hair, but quite a chipper fellow. I asked him what he did to retain his sunny disposition. 'Well, I'll tell you,' he said. 'Every morning I get up and I make a choice to be happy that day.'"

Groucho was holding on to his cigar for a long time, but he never smoked it, he only sniffed it occasionally. "Everybody has their own Laurel and Hardy," he mused. "A miniature Laurel and Hardy, one on each shoulder. Your little Oliver Hardy bawls you out—he says, 'Well, this is a fine mess you've gotten us into.' And your little Stan Laurel gets all weepy— 'Oh, Ollie, I couldn't help it. I'm sorry, I did the best I could....'"

Later, when Groucho started chuckling to himself, I hesitated to interrupt his reverie, but I had to ask, "What struck you funny?"

"I was thinking about this movie, Skidoo," he said. "I mean some of it is just plain ridiculous. This kid puts his stationery, which is soaked in LSD, into the water supply of the prison, and suddenly everybody gets completely reformed. There's a prisoner who says, 'Oh, gosh, now I don't have to be a rapist any more!' But it's also sophisticated in its own way. I like how Jackie Gleason, the character he plays, accepts the fact that he's not the biological father of his daughter."

"Oh, yeah? That sounds like the ultimate ego loss."

"But I'm really getting a big kick out of playing somebody named God like a dirty old man. You wanna know why?"

"Typecasting?"

"No, no—it's because—do you realize that irreverence and reverence are the same thing?"

"Always?"

"If they're not, then it's a misuse of your power to make people laugh." His eyes began to tear. "That's funny," he said. "I'm not even sad."

Then he went to urinate. When he came back, he said, "You know, everybody is waiting for miracles to happen. But the whole human body is a goddamn miracle."

He recalled Otto Preminger telling him about his own response to taking LSD and then he mimicked Preminger's accent: "I saw tings, bot I did not zee myself." Groucho was looking in a mirror on the dining room wall, and he said, "Well, I can see myself, but I still don't understand what the hell I'm doing here...."

A week later, Groucho told me that the Hog Farm had turned him on with marijuana on the set of Skidoo.

"You know," I said, "my mother once warned me that LSD would lead to pot."

"Well, your mother was right."

When Skidoo was released, Tim Leary saw it, and he cheerfully admitted, "I was fooled by Otto Preminger. He's much hipper than me."

The last time I saw Groucho was in 1976. He was speaking at the Los Angeles Book Fair. He looked frail and unsmiling, but he was alert and irascible as ever. He took questions from the audience.

"Are you working on a film now?"

"No, I'm answering silly questions.

"What are your favorite films?"

"Duck Soup. Night at the Opera."

"What do you think about Richard Nixon?"
"He should be in jail."
"Is humor an important issue in the presidential campaign?"
"Get your finger out of your mouth."
"What do you dream about?"
"Not about you."
"What inspired you to write?"
"A fountain pen. A piece of paper."

Then I called out a question: "What gives you the most optimism?"

I expected him to say "People" again, but this time he said, "The world."

There was hardly any standing room left in the auditorium, yet one fellow was sitting on the floor rather than take the aisle seat occupied by a large Groucho Marx doll.

James Lee Jobe

The Revolution of James Lee Jobe

It just so happens
that I'm planning a revolution.
It's going to start right here.
With me.

This is not a revolution with guns
or hidden bombs or hijackings.
There will be no attacks or assassinations,
no one will be robbed or shot or kidnapped.
A Revolution without tears!
Without blood!

And this is not a revolution to conquer
or to seize power, or to replace one tyranny
with another. No one will run wild in the streets.
The government will not be toppled, the banks
will not be seized. We will not trade
hatred for hatred.

Those are the very things that enslave us.

Now is the time to lay down all arms,
the whole world over! We need them
to love each other for the radiant soul
that we each carry inside.
Power will no longer rule, our hearts will.
Strength will not be measured by deaths
or even births, but by the love
we allow to enter our souls!

Your soul is a hermit crab
in need of room to grow, searching
for a new shell, and the ocean floor can be cold

and brutal. Do not give up the search, even though
it may take the entire length of your life. Crawl
across the ocean floor, through cold water
and brutality. This is your life!

This is the revolution of kindness,
the revolution of soul, our differences loved,
not fought over, no matter how anyone prays,

no matter how dark or light our skin, no matter
who we chose for a lover. Those who have
will reach out to those have not. Those who are full
will feed the hungry. Those with homes
will build homes for the homeless.
No child needs to know hunger or poverty.
And no person, no human being,
will be shamed.
And this is a revolution that will forgive
those who led us on the paths of violence
and ignorance, in hopes that their souls will open
and accept this forgiveness. Imagine
a planet of plenty and peace, a world paradise,
a world of neighbors, men and women
walking through the paces of life with faith
in the joy that is born inside of us;
this stands before us, brother, sister,
as sure as tomorrow's sunrise,
as sure as the pull of the moon on the ocean,
all we need do is stand up, together,
one people, one world,

renounce the hate that has ruled us
since time began.
Now.

Together.
I demand a new world! Sisters and brothers
joined by their hearts! Joy, wrapped into a bundle
and left on every doorstep. Food for every stomach,

salvation for any and all who reach for it, and a return
of hope to those who are living their lives in hard shadow.
Open your heart! Open your life!

It just so happens
that I'm planning a revolution.
It's going to start right here.
With me.

NL Centrum

David A. Ross

Like the interior of Vincent Van Gogh's studio, Willie Weber's visceral workplace was filled with empty bird's nests, old mud-stained shoes, broken chairs, fallen limbs, and filthy peasants' caps. Walking against the north wind from the Hotel America, he'd slipped inside the gray building on Amsterdam's Paulus Potterstraat and spent the afternoon with the dead artist. From every picture and drawing, from every letter, receipt, and scrap of hand-written paper, Vincent had whispered to him: "You cannot be at the pole and the equator at the same time. You must choose your own line...."

The rain was coming down again as Willie passed through the neighborhood known as the Jordaan. The narrow alleyways and timeworn, working class, brown brick houses gave the quarter a dank, enclosed feeling. Here souls tended to brood; and your neighbor was likely to be your aunt or your uncle.

As Willie navigated through the wet streets, he could hear a rock band practicing nearby. He stopped to listen, but the buildings were situated so closely together that it was impossible to trace the sound of the echo. Like a confused rat in a maze, he chased after phantom drumbeats and nebulous bass lines to no avail. He was about to abandon the search when a peeling guitar solo helped him zero in on the basement where the tumultuous music was boiling over with rage, desperation, dreams, and oblivion.

He walked down the cellar stairs to listen outside the door. The words were all in riotous Dutch, so Willie, a native German speaker, only vaguely understood their meaning; but the music was tough and hard, the notes and phrases condensed and wrapped tight as a bale of wire. These bloody and wounded drumbeats were as unnerving as an arrhythmic heartbeat, and a curious ensemble of techno-synthetic instruments seemed to be converging on some point of critical mass, at first catastrophic, then circling round to some implied reassurance.

Trying the door Willie found it not locked, and he boldly pushed it open. The chamber was mostly dark and smelled of hashish and whiskey. He squinted to see in this vat of murky water. Four phosphorescent eels swam in well-measured frequency through waves of tubular light. Like the avant-garde culture in which they lived, these four musicians were suspended in mid-song, like a team of trapeze artists caught with insufficient pendular momentum to execute a critical maneuver. For a time no one noticed him standing there. But as the song they were rehearsing finally degenerated into chaos, the sallow-faced, leather-clad singer approached him. The singer's knees nearly buckled under the weight of his own ruin, and his sense of direction was battered by some blitzkreig of distortion generators, bizarre harmonics, and drugs. Careening and glassy-eyed, he looked sickly in the smoky basement of Calvinism's worst nightmare.

"Daag!" he said.

"I don't mean to intrude," Willie apologized.

The young vocalist stared vacantly at him.

Willie asked, "Sprechen-sie Deutsch?"

"Ja, Ich spreche Deutsch," the singer smirked. "But since I was born in the Jardaan, some Hollanders say I don't even speak very good Dutch."

"I heard the music and came to listen," Willie said.

"Come inside," said the singer. Willie followed him into the crypt. "Where do you come from?" he asked.

"Der Stadt Erlangen—north of Nürnberg."

"Der Fatterland!"

The singer turned to his colleagues and recapped the conversation thus far in their own language.

"My name is Axel Van Zoet," he said.

"Willie Weber."

Each band member shook his hand.

"Are you sure you don't mind if I stay?" Willie asked.

"No problem," said Axel. He took a bottle of Teacher's from inside his leather jacket and offered Willie a drink.

"No, thanks," said Willie.

"You sure? It's okay, I don't care."

Willie declined.

Axel asked: "What brings you to Amsterdam? Hashish? Heroin? Other drugs?"

"Nothing so easy to find," said Willie. "Perhaps a rare piece of art—or just a memorable scene."

"The graffiti is good in Amsterdam," assessed Axel. "But real art—I mean art in the contemporary sense—too many clichés for art to survive."

"What are your lyrics about?" Willie asked.

"Stress."

"Stress?"

"Stress and tension. That's all." Axel offered the whiskey bottle again. "Are you some sort of artist?"

"I'm an engineer."

Willie's thoughts retreated to his recent past. He saw before him certain specs of a motor he had once designed to drive a gimbal, or to move an optical lens—Element #6 for the Laser Doppler Rangefinder. It was later sold to the American Defense Department, he learned. In the beginning, those for whom he'd worked would not verify the motor's true purpose; they were vague and evasive—an insult to his intelligence and his creativity, which they supposedly valued. Many times he'd asked that they simply tell him the truth, but they had not.

"I'm trained as an architect," Axel revealed, "but for now I prefer to fuck around with this music. Fewer constraints, more room for expression."

Willie nodded.

"What kind of art are you searching for?" the iconoclast wanted to know. "Do you mean Rembrandt? Everybody who comes to the Netherlands wants to see Rembrandt and Van Gogh. But there are other possibilities."

"I've seen the Van Gogh collection," said Willie.

"Look!" said Axel. "Maybe you would like to go with me tomorrow night to see something very unusual. Art with a real impact! It involves sculpture, mechanics, and theater all at once. This group of artists—or maybe like yourself they are actually engineers—is doing something unique, I believe."

Putting caution aside, Willie said, "Warum nicht?"

Axel smiled for the first time. "Meet me here tomorrow evening at seven o'clock. First we'll go to Café Chris for supper, and then we'll go to Mickery Theater. I know you won't be disappointed, Willie Weber."

To Theo's frustration, Vincent was forever giving away his small stipend to those less fortunate than he—if indeed such persons were to be found! Left alone in Arles by the artist Paul Gaugin, misunderstood and suffering seizures and blackouts, Vincent preferred oblivion to the constant fear of epilepsy, and shot himself point blank in the stomach. Mortally wounded, he lay on his bed, bleeding, and smoked his pipe. Fragrant wreaths of smoke gathered in swirling clouds about his head, and the painter died amidst his own yellow vision.

Shortly after dark, Willie left his room at the Hotel America with flexuous Van Goth visions freshly imprinted on his mind: crows and wheat fields, dour and oblique-looking peasants eating potatoes, terrace cafés, Vincent's bedroom, landscapes, skeletons, and the red and green and orange portrait of the artist himself, his ear bandaged, and looking quite mad. Outside it was raining again, and he walked quickly across Daam Square. Taking refuge from the mist in a cozy tavern, he ordered a beer and sat down at a corner table. The smoke from the cigarettes and pipes of a dozen other drinkers filtered out the clarity he sought to invoke.

And yes, he'd made an unlikely engagement for tomorrow night with the punk singer-architect, Axel Van Zoet. He had no idea what to expect. That was fine. Willie took a sip of his beer. Then another. He looked at his palms and discovered that they were stained with the oil pigments of the primary colors—some reactionary stigmata. He bit his lower lip in reflection and searched for help. No one in the tavern saw the tears falling from his eyes.

Café Chris had been in business on the Bloemstraat as a beer tap since 1624. Axel Van Zoet's studio was located just a few blocks away. Outside the café a spray of purple tulips grew in a window box and set off the clean lines of the well-maintained building. Red, full-length drapes hung inside the windows, complimenting perfectly the design of the dark green, wrought iron trim. The interior was finished with dark wood paneling. The lighting was subdued. Willie offered to buy dinner for his host. Axel was a little surprised, but he did not decline Willie's offer to pay.

"Look," he said. "This isn't much of a place. Only simple food and good beer."

"Seems fine to me," said Willie.

They took seats in a far corner of the tapperij. There were no menus, only four pre-determined suppers written in Dutch on a blackboard behind the bar. Axel translated the possibilities for Willie, and the guest settled on a mushroom omelet with grilled onions. Axel ordered a crock of fish stew with brown bread. They each had draught beer.

As Axel lit a cigarette, Willie examined his companion's features. Axel's sallow face and pointed chin and hollow cheeks suggested simple artistic poverty. And his dyed, jet-black hair was long and scruffy at the neck, while cut short and unevenly at the temples. He had a defiant cowlick on the crown of his head. Underneath his black leather jacket, he wore a t-shirt with faded lettering that read, "NL Centrum."

"Amsterdam is small scale," he said without prompting. "Very domestic, very complacent. Of course all the so-called hippies would have you believe it's very chic. It's not that at all. Here in Amsterdam, we live very close together. That is the real reason for civility."

"To an outsider, it appears as if nobody's actually in control," Willie observed.

"Yes! Now you've touched the real issue," said Axel, quite pleased. "Look, there are many forms of control, as there are many variations of freedom. In any society, freedom is only control by degrees. That's what we're really talking about."

"I'm not sure I follow you."

"Let me explain. Amsterdam is the great experiment in controlling people by giving them everything they want. If you want hashish or pot, they say go ahead, it's okay. If you want heroin or cocaine, they look the other way. Sex? Here it's lost all enchantment. In the end it all comes down to economics. Same as Deutschland, or England, or Japan, or America—a colossal commercial, that's it!"

"So you're opposed to liberalism?"

"Look, sooner or later the pendulum will swing back the other way. It's predictable. Right? Left? But it's all a great distraction, isn't it? Meanwhile, fundamental issues are ignored. But on a grander scale—a worldwide scale—tension is building. Don't you feel it?"

"We're all pawns: Is that what you're saying?"

Axel shrugged as he filled his mouth with stew.

"As an engineer in Germany, I thought I was working on a weather radar system. As it turned out, my work was subverted."

"So that's why you're in Amsterdam?" Axel queried.

"I don't really know why I'm here," said Willie.

Axel moved closer, putting his face just inches away from Willie's. "Look, if you stay here awhile, you'll begin to see that it's no different. A grand seduction, that's it! All the hippies are lapsing into comas, and the punks are kicking ass and screaming anarchy! There's no anarchy. It's only made to resemble anarchy. What's really going on is control. It's compliance invoked by seduction!"

Seduced by promises of recompense both direct and subliminal, bribes and rewards that, once attained, never quite satisfied, the perverse feeling of emptiness that resulted grew slowly but steadily into an accustomed, dull ache, and no longer had Willie Weber been willing to chase after phantom redress. There had to be something more—something that might restore a measure of dignity!

After dinner they headed for Mickery Theater.

The night was damp and the wind blew relentlessly off the waterfront. The arched pedestrian bridges were outlined with strings of tiny, white fantasy lights, and many of the boats and stately old canal houses were lit as well.

"Just what is it we're about to see?" Willie asked Axel.

"It's a performance by a consortium called Survival Research Laboratories, or SRL for short."

"Sounds serious," said Willie.

Well, it is and it isn't. It's a metaphor, yes. But it also tries to stand all on its own. You see, the world theater maintains drama and tension through the perpetuation of greed and injustice and so forth. In this allegory, everything comes crashing down. So these performances are about creating more problems than they solve. Yes, it is theater with machines as characters, and each time the audience must be sacrificed!"

Before four hundred open-mouthed onlookers, Mickery Theater was transformed by the members of Survival Research Laboratories into something resembling a prehistoric chasm populated by nightmarish, four-meter-high, mechanical creatures: steel dinosaurs, friction threshers, shock wave cannons, erector set mania. Born of inverse ingenuity and a blow torch mentality, these fortified joints and welded junctures, these dancing skeletons, flame throwers, dolts, and catapults were apparently built only to collapse upon themselves. Their mechanical sounds were primordial: shattering glass, fire bombs, cargo exploding, scaffolding crashing, animal outcries

In a collective movement, the audience recoiled as huge booms swung out over the first twenty rows, spreading scraps of fetid refuse. Loud speakers barked unintelligible castigation at one hundred fifty decibels. Axel Van Zoet, the die-hard rock musician, covered his ears and grimaced, while the girl standing beside him tugged tensely at her hair. All the while, the shock wave cannon fired wake-up calls at the audience. Rancid debris rained down like nuclear fallout. Willie laughed uneasily, but as the performance continued he came to realize that the creators of this theatrical whatever-it-was were engineers, and this was their personal dare with the world!

"We're witnessing the technocratic world at war with itself," Willie yelled in Axel's ear as Armageddon thundered onstage.

"Yes, but it becomes even more!" Axel observed. "These machines are at ease in the world the artists have created for them. They take on a life all their own. Ultimately, the personality of the machine exceeds that of its operator."

Here no status quo expressions of talent were manifest. Each person who saw the performance was challenged to make up his own story about what was happening right in front of his eyes. A successful performance meant the development of new idioms!

"I can't imagine a production like this taking place in Germany," Willie told Axel. "The polizei would close it down in minutes."

"Perhaps they would not understand it," suggested Axel.

"On the contrary," said Willie, "I'm afraid they'd understand it all too well."

Once the performance ended the crowd filed out of Mickery Theater, but they did not immediately disperse. Instead, they stood outside the auditorium, waiting for the world to end. And for a new one to begin. Word began circulating that SRL's fire cannon had been stolen. "With their consent, I suspect," Axel said with a self-satisfied look on his face. "Though of course they'll never admit it."

Willie stood by his new friend.

Minutes later they heard a low-pitched hum, followed by several muted popping sounds. In time they could see clouds of billowing black smoke rising into the chilly night air. Scores of police were running in the direction of the commotion.

"I knew something was bound to happen," commented Axel.

"I don't understand," said Willie. "What is it?"

"Five minutes walk from here there was a long-time squat. Not anymore."

For they'd burned the entire ghetto to the ground!

Deena Remiel

Permission Granted to Succeed

barriers
seen and heard
in our faces and traces of our words
felt and absorbed
into the very fabric of our being
to fester and spread like a terminal disease
self-inflicted wounds that never heal
we have been taught
how to fear the possible
how to doubt the plausible
how to deny the tangible
our souls are imprisoned
our spirits, immobilized
where to go?
where to grow?
 from one tiny seed, a bit of praise
a single nugget of encouragement
is allowed entry to our hearts
and another still, releasing the shackles
one agonizing beat at a time
 until
courage replaces the fear
belief replaces the doubt
and acceptance replaces the denial
permission granted to succeed

Deena Remiel

Connections

Invisible threads tether us, one to another
as a lifeline to substantiate our existence
to validate our voices, our choices
 A community of isolated souls
beseeching, and reaching for inclusion
casting aside skepticism in favor of belief
 We fit, we feel
the sameness and saneness in our lives
we laugh and cajole
knowing our role is to support and celebrate
our small victories, and our large successes
 A finely woven cloth, we are
made of different colors, textures
creating a most unique fabric
 connections
a knowing, and growing
of the human spirit.

Deena Remiel

In-

Insufficient
Insincere
Indifferent
Inexcusable
Inadequate
Inattentive
Insensitive
Insolent
Intolerable
In denial

Timothy Gager

Sam Jesus in the Tub

On acid they were a tribe
worshipping a soapstone god
with hymns sounding more
like Pink Floyd's Division Bell
than Holy, Holy, Holy.

Waters of violet overflow
the bathtub's like a womb with
six knees and elbows,
four breasts, one cock crowing,
bathed in wet vestments
for the Almighty
leading to confessional prayers
during this mass;
a part of the period
waiting and preparing
for the Second Coming

Timothy Gager

Why We Listen to the Universe

It'll tell you what
you should head toward and
what you should follow.
Which leads me from me to you,
to which I say,
it is ok to be alone.

The trees are alone,
the air is as well,
the sea is not needy
and we do not ask of the sea.

The universe prepares
us to die, we move each day,
the soul being singular, even
the phrase "we are at one
with the Universe" is wrong.
People still hope, beg, wish
for being "at two" because

    inside they are an empty hole

    waiting to be filled with dirt.

Still I ask It about loneliness,
about the things I don't have,
and it shows me that I am a stupid man,
just a boy again—the Universe has led
me to you, tells me….it's ok.
see the trees, breathe the air, listen
to the waves of the ocean.

Timothy Gager

To Care About Life

      god will not roll the dice
but he is there on a cross around your neck,
not to protect but to strangle you,
with his strong finger just to keep you alive.

the stream that licks your toes today

      will eventually dry, no fish left to catch

      when you need to cast your line,
the tributaries become thinner

      and thinner, like veins collapsing,

      you'll leave your own ocean unreached,
unfulfilled, as wasteful as knowing,
the ending of life's book where.

We wait for those fish to die,
but you should dance in the receding water.

Timothy Gager

After Smoking Dope

We had lunch at Pizzapalooza
made us think, how
many other spin offs
are there?

So, my friend Fred
who knows a lot of things
about a lot of things said
Polar Palooza, then
Pet-a-Palooza, of course
Learn-A-Palooza and
don't forget Puf-a-Palooza,
a 15-hour marathon
of vintage Sid and Marty Krofft
productions. dude, we said,
what-the-fuck-are-you-a loser?

Then my date aspirated
but Fred knew
the Heimlich Maneuver
as she choked, the wind ruffled
in the trees outside
until a leaf spiraled off,
just like that.

Laura Strathman Hulka

Cancer Dancer

The News. The Trance
Cellular rebellion
Reality, acceptance, thus it begins,
The Dance

I am a Cancer Dancer...
Not my definition, but how can I sway to this unknown tango,
Without letting the disease take hold in heart and soul?

I am a Cancer Dancer....
Spinning on metaphorical toes.
Surgery: An emptiness of gut, allowing
the newly hollowed places to fill with
different steps and rhythms.

I am a Cancer Dancer...
Learning anew, tapping the sacred healing drum to draw
its resonance inside...touching scarred tissue.
I am open to the healing of the goddess

I am a Cancer Dancer...
Enveloped in mindfulness,
creating far flung and frantic steps to
make the chemo move
quickly throughout my beleaguered body

I am a Cancer Dancer...
Avoiding labels, refusing boxes,
wanting instead the aura of peaceful choices.
Arms held akimbo, eyes closed, feet moving,
gliding, rarely faltering.

I am a Cancer Dancer

Opening to new forms of dance, of being...
Anxiously eager to embrace bright vital newness
of ideas and desires. I am being born with fresh chances ~~
The Phoenix, The Chameleon, The Snake.
I am HERE.

Lyn Lifshin

Montmartre

Haven't you wanted, sometimes, to
walk into some painting, start a new
life? The quiet blues of Monet would
soothe but I don't know how long I'd
want to stay there. Today I'm in the
mood for something more lively,
say Lautrec's Demimonde. I want
that glitter, heavy sequin nights.
You take the yellow sunshine for
tonight. I want the club scene
that takes you out all night. Come
on, wouldn't you, just for a night or
two? Gaslights and absinthe, even
the queasy night after dawn. Wouldn't
you like to walk into Montmartre
where everything you did or
imagined doing was de rigueur,
pre-Aids with the drinkers and
artists and whores? Don't be so P.C.,
so righteous you'd tell me you haven't
imagined this? Give me the Circus
Fernando, streets where getting stoned
was easy and dancing girls kick high.
It's just the other side of the canvas,
the thug life, a little lust. It was good
enough for Van Gogh and Lautrec,
Picasso. Can't you hear Satie on the
piano? You won't be able to miss
Toulouse, bulbous lips, drool. Could
you turn down a night where glee
and strangeness is wide open? Think
of Bob Dylan leaving Hibbing. A little
decadence can't hurt. I want the swirl

of cloth under changing colored lights,
nothing square, nothing safe, want to
can can thru Paris, parting animal
nights, knees you can't wait
to taste flashing

Lyn Lifshin

Door Mat

I can still remember how
annoyed she got the first time
I used it, "Door mat,"
the way her mother let a brute
of a man walk all over her.
"Door mat"—you'd think I
called her mother whore or
bitch. Not strange, I went on,
so many women are at times.
I started a list of them: the
ones who faked orgasm to
keep some man, the ones who
say nothing when strangers
look and call their husbands,
"charming, so nice." Door mat
I say. I like the word. The ones
someone else wipes their feet,
their penis all over: what
woman I want to say without a
job, a good job and kids hasn't
had a stint keeping her mouth shut,.
making excuses. One friend has
taken to buying cheap sexy
clothes, bustiers and fish
net instead of painting. Door
mat, dour mat. **Door mat**
I want to scream at my
aunt who coddles her 45
year old son who probably
steels her money. Even Hilary
was, I hiss, standing up for
him with his penis in who
knows whose mouth. I want

to say, maybe because I feel
so tired and hardly an Amazon
today, walking about, some
one not me, afraid like all the
other D.M's to say what I
am really thinking

Lyn Lifshin

After The Tsunami

some are still crying,
some come to weep
but no tears come. Some
have lost everyone.
For some, this dooms
day was more than their
minds could bear. In the
middle of rubble, a
young woman named
Nofal sits on the low wall
everyday wrapped in a
blanket and sings. She
has gone mad. In her wild
eyes and laughter that
seems to come from some
deep dreadful place she
sings everyone's song.
"All is destroyed. My
family, 8 or 9 people. All
gone, no more. I have no
phone. 45579, that's my
phone number."

Lyn Lifshin

Spiritual

Have you noticed anything about
those who describe themselves
or their writing or painting as
spiritual? Do you cringe, as some
might at the words "fuck" or
"shit?" that, tho maybe crude,
don't offend me? The "spiritual"
aren't able to say them, out-loud
at least. There's something about
the ones who say they are, like
others who say they're so glad they
live in the north or south or east
or west where people are lovelier,
imply of course that you probably
aren't. I notice those who keep
praising their spirituality say
you don't understand suggesting
it is because you aren't. But I
notice these "spiritual" people often
aren't. Isn't it phony to gush what
a godly person you are and then
dream a banishment room for your
husband, care more about money
you are making than about much
else. When the spiritual gush, does
your skin crawl too? Those
Pollyannas you could never be,
forget the mystical. And when they
end their e mail with "life is good
and it gets better every day if you
think it is," don't you just
want to go and take a bath?

Lyn Lifshin

He's Moved Everything He Needs Into One Room

walls of books on
the Holocaust, revolutions,
Iraq and Nam block
the light. Paper from
D-Day, divorce
papers with stains of cups
all over. The velvet
zip bag of medals, part
of the moat around the
mattress he's
curled on under
a brushed cotton quilt:
you couldn't call any
thing in this room
a comforter. Crumbs
from the last three
weeks, machete
in a top drawer, machine
guns, a 44. Librium
crumbled near ashes,
punching bag, the
insides spill out
of like *entrails
in the jungle* he said
*I took the man's
intestines, washed them
off in rain water,
stuffed them back into
the slit like
squeezing bread
crumbs into a turkey*

Andrew J Pensabene, III

No Mad

I am jesus, I am, I am,
in the navy once too,
excuse me, got a smoke

No, get away! (passerby)

(Walking, limp & spits) horses petute,
petudie, duty, nudie...(sic)
my fathers naked noah
on a crutch,
his donkey's broken,
busted, dust.

(Stop, Sit)
Stinking
Ah but its like
nutmeg.
Ma, heres to you...
Top of the world,
top of toes, nose, shhh (eyes close):

(Store owner) Hey buddy wake up,
com'on, you can't sleep here,
(kicks) hey get up.
I got to open up...

(School girls late for class) eeuuu
Look, it's soooo dirty,
Dis gus sting
Ehhh...(tongue receives finger)
Oh My god, it smells like pee...
Hurry...

(Waking)

Hey i'm jeez usss
how you squeeze us,
pray, play with me...
Yo, gotta smoke...(finger curling)
Com'ere little gurrrls...

(Store owner)
Hey, you talk like that again
and I'll have you arrested...

(Stares hotly)
I'm in the bigger jail,
biggest jail... (twitch)
You open (almost lucid)
I need a drink,
just back from
a Bushmans breakfast...

(Store owner)
You got money...

(Staring, burning)
Yeah, here,
crumpled bills and
grimy coins...

(Store owner)
First you drink water,
then you can buy, OK, buddy.
You come by every day,
you stink...
Why don't you get cleaned up,
you sleep on the streets,
whats the matter with you?

(Laval eyes, lasers fire)
Eh, soap is so slutty,

I won the lotto

and

don't want to pay taxes.
I hate the government...
War and fat pigs...
They do what they want...
Everyones insects,
ya know,
its just how I see'em!

(Head shaking stops, tilts,
only the whites of his eyes show,
shining, waiting for agreement)

(Store Owner)
You know buddy
you're crazy
get some help.
Here's your change.

Andrew J Pensabene, III

Snaps

Snaps Into peas and dragons
with pop and crackle to follow
under princess' mattress'
and jolly green fellows,
festive but straight
to the crash then catch
released by law and size
the sport of spine
made from old an dust...

As once the earth was covered

miles high in rainbow colored mats
orange blues greens purples and reds
algae prokaryotes
each on an atoms track spewing
pollutions action
following elemental paths.
Sky became poison
killing whole generations of
thousands of years in the making
the first ghost emerges.

Cells without center
began to succumb under pressure
and folded into each other
protecting against ultra violets
let in by an oxygen rich lens
as wounds became wombs when touched
bandages became sex
instead of viral copy

membranes arranged
around a nucleus
giving birth to cellular union

Out of survival, death
or the phantom limbs itch
DNA shifts gears and gains
another rung on the way
to your brain...

reading each line of text
which wanted to start with
yo mama's so big,
K mart had to change "One size fit's all"
to "One size fits most"
when she stood up she covered the sun
which darkened the page
and snatched the next thought
out my head
to end this piece up with
with a whimper not a Dang.

Ernest Stewart

Sausalito

Wish I was back in California,
Away from this Michigan snow and ice.
Back where I'd be simple and free.
Away from this Michigan winter life.

Wish I was home in Sausalito,
Laying with my lady by the bay.
Back where we'd be simple and free
and there we'd live and love the livelong day.

If I get back to California,
I'm going to stay there Lord and never more roam.
Back where we'd be, happy and free,
there in our California home.

Wish I was back in California.
Away from this Michigan snow and ice.
Back where I'd be simple and free.
Away from this Michigan winter life.

Ernest Stewart

The Drums Of War

The drums of war ring loud tonight
The traitor's words ring hollow.
To steal some oil they'll go and fight
But I will never follow.

The golden land of yesterday
Is gone forever more.
And from the ashes sad to say
Arises the Phoenix of war.

A lie is told, the truth is spun
One thousand die a day.
Till every loving mother's son
Is fighting in the fray.

The years pass by without a change
Except the deadly score.
And still they try to rearrange
To kill a million more.

What goes around, will come around
Someday upon our shore.
Prometheus will come, unbound
To even up the score.

Empires rise, empires fall
And ours will do the same.
It's not how high you build the wall
But how you play the game!

Hans Plomp

No Guru

Wherever we look, wherever we go,
God the Father leads the show.
Tell me father, tell me son,
where have all our Goddesses gone?
No father, for me, no guru!
No Jesus, no Mao, no Marx, no Buddha,
no Satan, no Krishna, no Zarathustra.
No leaders down here or up above,
I just want Great Lady Love.
Women of the universe,
only you can end this curse.
Freya, Venus, Durga, Isis,
ladies why do you allow this?
Please come back and show your face,
bring this stinking world some grace.
We don't need no virgin mother,
We don't need no tyrant father,
We don't need no crucified son,
We need Woman!

We need Love Wisdom Justice
the Triple Goddess.
We need boundless beauty
to clean up the mess.
No Moloch, no Kronos, no Baal, no Allah,
but Lakshmi, Minerva, and ancient Inanna.
No leaders on earth or in heaven above,
but you forever, Lady Love.

Hans Plomp

"Reach inside ... "

Reach inside
for your fondest dream:
make it grow, make it strong,
turn it into poetry or song.
Out there, in reality,
look for your dream's company.
Surely there are spirits here
who will hold the same dream dear.
This is life's creative core.
This is what I'm living for.

Michael Rothenberg

Choose

I have a clue
Monkeys like to be left alone

They don't smoke cigars or play poker
Prefer not to dress up like The Three Bears
But a man's got to do what a man's got to do

Sunflower seeds, bananas, peanuts
Making industry out of ecology
10,000 years of giving up
Now we're supposed to compromise

So we take what's left and split it
Take what's left and split
Until everything is in ownership

And no one can live
Because there are too many fences
Up to the moon and across the cosmos

Michael Rothenberg

Seven Days In Darien

Spanish moss, Live oaks, resurrection ferns
Fort King George Motel
Reading *Baghavad Gita*
Todd reads the turtle news
"Leatherback Nesting on Sapelo Island"
Apple passion fruit juice, peanut butter cookies
Shower, shave, and go to sleep

An American gator drifts down the river
Bottlenose dolphins roil

At 10 a.m meet Sinkey Boone, shrimp fisherman
At the Waffle House for grits

Fishermen and environmentalists talk
About turtle excluder device
By-catch, aqua-culture, sodium dip
Marketing links, Georgia
Sweet browns, whites and pinks

Whelk shell heap glares in the hot noon sun

We visit Fort King George Historic Site
Tidal mills, saw blades, stockades, brick ruins
Guale Indians, French, Scottish, British
The Church fought for control of Altamaha Delta

Corn snake. Indigo snake
Ibis, egret, bunting
Cabbage palm, palmetto and holly

At the Buccaneer Club
Lunch of boiled shrimp

Hushpuppies and French fries

More talk about sea turtle strandings
Sea turtles caught in shrimp nets
Mutilated in Texas, drowned in Georgia
No one has an answer

"It isn't the fisherman's fault," says Sinkey
"We're sea farmers in Sea Gardens."

I remember poaching loggerheads
in Everglades National Park 35 years ago
Butchered on the sand spit at night
The bloody heart and gutted carapace

Survey soft sand hills with Sinkey
Slash pine forests and cypress swamp
Find alligator skeleton and teeth
Todd roots and turns rotted wood
I sit on the banks and twirl a doodle-bug stick

Lake ripples lap the shore willows
Sand-fleas bite my bare ankles
Orange velvet ants investigate the ground
Herons wade. Mullets leap
A small bird with a pretty song
No one can identify

Mangrove seeds drift over oyster beds
Smilax thickets and bald cypress
Tangles of Muscadine vines
We climb a big old tree to look over
Miles and miles of cord grass marshlands

On the shrimp boat "Bertha"
Equipped with Turtle Excluder Device
The captain cooks us Certified Turtle Safe♩ sea bobs
Pinches off their heads

Adds a bottle of medium hot salsa
Squirt of liquid margarine
Salt and pepper
Boil until pink
The shells pop right off
We eat four pounds

St. Simon's Island Festival
Washboard thumping, bass singing, "Oh, When the Saints…"
Deviled-crabs, barbecued ribs, smoked mullet
And sweet potato pie

We visit the vacant pond habitat of Wally
A pet alligator shot in the face by vandals

Bright blue tailed skink species
expecatus or *fasciatus* iridescent in a wood pile

Vultures on turtle carcass hill
Pink sunset splash

At Day's Inn in Jacksonville
Waves of discovery and no answers
I think we ought to boycott shrimp
Todd disagrees
The next day fly to Boston
Leave a note for Todd, "Save the Turtles"
Remember Darien

Jesse Mitchell

Bodhi Tree

The evening is the music
The music that we hear.
the rhythm, a pounding drum
The night is the sound.
And noise and pieces of muttered mumbled
And shuttered shakings.
above is jazz
And the sky is that reflection
And the stars the dance
Of things below.
The bodhi tree quivers on the brink of war.
Dark green velvet shakes and shakes
And shakes
The cool wet dew
The soft drops
On the verge of violence
Shake.
The Bodhi tree quivers on the edge of silence
Shattered
By the movement
The movement above…
The reflection below.
above is jazz
And the sky is that reflection
And the stars the dance
Of things below.
Twist and turn
Sparkle, gleam,
And burn.
The Bodhi tree quivers on the brink of war.

Jesse Mitchell

Orbit

In the green semi circle line
Line of green trees.
In front and middle of beaming glowing yellow light
And bursting white…the bursting luminescent white…
Soaking wet words hang in the air
Words hang above in the moist mumbled air…
Lost crumbled air
the broken and busted
Building
Nothing but a Shed
with
Holes in the floor
Cracks in the holy roof
Everything
Hanging in the clouds
Constructed by magic
Constructed in magic
In the sky above.
The sides falling in
Lines once plumb and straight
Angles and lines
All the mathematical
And religious things
And places
And hiding
Saints in the shadows
Shadows of light
Light filled with shadows and pause.
Light running in though

The cracks and breaks
Light filled with bubbles and dust
And angels and esoteric things
Light filled light
Filling a light starved dark
In the middle of a
Color bled
Curve
In the middle of a water soaked
Line
Of sky
And light
Escaping
The eye.

Michelle Close Mills

Shoes

In times of trial,
we find ourselves
not knowing what to do,
or which way to go.
In the midst of confusion,
it's easy to block
the needs of those
around us...
looking instead on
our angst,
and our pain.
But giving
to others
who need who we are,
helps us to find peace

in our hearts
and our lives.

Redirecting our pain
by easing another's,
makes our own pain
much lighter...
we find reasons for joy...
newly blessed by all
we've been given.
In walking a mile
in another man's shoes,
we have the chance to relearn
the gratitude for
the perfect fit
of our own.

Michelle Close Mills

The Void
(an Army wife's lament)

Everyone thinks
I'm the girl to
go to...
the one who has
her head on straight.
Who has been there,
done that...
who can mend anything...
If they only knew
how screwed up
I am.
Aching, forlorn...
far away
from my heart,

which is held by
the one who
loves me
best of all.
I'm enveloped
by people
who are
droning their words.
I try to join in...
to appear just
like them...
but inside I'm as
as cold as
the grave.
There's a
vast gaping void
that once brimmed

with joy…
Now I am lost,

and alone,
cast adrift in the sea
of a life that once was

full of hope,
and delight.
I'm begging,
I'm pleading
for you to return…
Bring my heart
and come home
to me.

I need you.

Martha Meltzer

A Good Hippie Had No Last Name

That summer we were Dana and Lennie
Deever and Turtle AJ and Big Bob
someone's old man or old lady
We lived together changing partners as the solstice moon
passed from one phase to the next
Home was canyon cabins where coyotes howled
or back houses within the sound of the sea
We slept on mattresses on floors windows open to catch a breeze
Patchouli and pot smoke drifting out as we passed a joint
Vegan and carnivore a tab under our tongue
we drank cheap red wine straight from gallon jugs
Bearded braless long hair blowing thumbs in the air
we traveled along making love not war
carrying our earthly possessions in Army/Navy surplus duffels
When we needed guidance we threw the I Ching
cast each other's horoscopes or read Tarot cards
It didn't matter where we were from or where we were going
We were restless and political   passionate and naïve
so rooted in conviction   the now of it all
consumed with summer possibilities
we didn't notice when the winds shifted
and an autumn breeze began to blow

Louise Levi

I Was Hitch Hiking Fr. Bagnore

I was hitchhiking in Castel del piano. A village boy picked me up/
great music in the car. 'Sonic Youth. He couldn't believe it when I
said *O yea' Thurston is a friend of mine*. He begged me to come to
a concert of SY in No. Italy/a Communist Festival/ A strange person
was among his friends.
Thurston gave us all free tickets & I became a
friend of the stranger. I used to see him

walking barefoot in the next village/ he had 'soul'.
real 'soul' — He'd cut off all his hair & lain it
in his mother's casket — he was the
'village stranger.'

One day he took me to a secret place behind
the village-a Japanese like wood where 2 deer & 2
peacocks were encaged/ I immediately felt the peacocks were
guardians & used to go to that forest to >practice'
(meditation); I always got a rush fr. the boy & sometimes had lunch
w.
him
&
his
sister.

I never cld. 'meditate at the 'center/
too much tension & 'hype'

*

Years later, S becomes a thief, a real
professional/ I never loved him less/ his father committed suicide/
but S. was sure it was assassination or 'black magic'/ His family
blamed him for his mother's death/a friend in the next town/an

elegant old man/ Valentino, turned out to be his grandfather/
maybe S. & I had old ties. He took me to all the right places/ he cld.
read my mind. His girlfriend got him into O./then blamed him &
made it impossible for him to see his son./ I wished he'd escaped to
India, the whole town did/ Instead, after >The Great Bank Robbery'
he basically turned himself
in/ couldn't do w/o the village/ He was a shaman/
/only shamans suffer
so much pain.

                                            even
migratory birds,
                 seek shelter, but where, one
night, in the arms of the night, I found
myself in a new terrain, birds were singing
but I cld. not hear them, the heavens
were veiling me, the heavens
who were to receive me,
instead descended
upon me—
I
knew the sheltered
land was near, I called in faint

voice, did you hear me? that night of
beginnings, that night of climax, that
night of reversal   universal,
the call, high in the
mountain,
a
single sleeping
angel, a lake of dew, somewhere
in the distance, your
name,
    your   name

David Meltzer

Ecocide

Ecocide is how
capitalism does
genocide

Too bad they don't get it
the part about the end

Stephen Lewandowski

Asleep In The Buddha

When I visit
she puts me in the spare room
with a bed, a desk, her books,
two meditation pillows and a brass Buddha.
The room is warm—I need only a light blanket—
and its walls are white.
Over the bed hangs a mandala.
Siamese cats visit me in the night.

Waking up, floor boards under my feet,
Gotama greets, one hand raised.
Bronze of the bell hanging beside his shrine
holds a long, singing note.
Dieffenbachia roots in a glass, blind
white rootlets, leaf arches over the Buddha.

A woodcut shows a gigantic man
smiling and directing a tiny traveler.
He is a traveler because his things
are done up in a bum's knotted handkerchief.
He is tiny because the giant is pointing
to a distant mountain.

I've come with Snyder's *Fudo*
and a beefsteak begonia to give away.
That done, I feel myself becoming tinier yet;
o white walls, white ceiling
brass Buddha setting on wood,
that mountain is huge
and so far away;
can't I stay here with you?

Stephen Lewandowski

Bedrock

Laid down layer by
layer of sediment
eroded from the landmass
and raining onto seabed over
whole colonies of Fenestella and Polypora
Neospirifera and Rhipidomella
shapes impressed in the mud shower

hills thrust above the water
and set on edge
their weak places washed away,
joints eroding and scattered
pressure heaving them higher
even as they wear down

ground by great icesheets
advance and retreat
gobs of sediment adhering
to the glacier's sole and
scouring the exposed bedrock
high places made low again
chunks cracked out of
the bed by frost, tumbling
down a bank from the gully
hidden in hemlock growth

and washed with the stream
flow of mud, stone, debris
settling into
an alluvium
a hayfield
where we sit for a music festival
afternoon stretching into the evening

the stones are hard
on our comfort, no place
to take it easy without
a point in your rib or hip
so a prize is offered
for the best stone sculpture

dancing couples and groups
a solo here and there
moving to rhythms
of the world music
some comb the site
for materials

300 million year old stone
washed and ground 10,000 years
a child picks up one, then another,
examines them closely
for a hidden shape
then makes the form of a hawk
castle turtle rocket bear

Geri Digiorno

Janis Joplin

her whiskey voice
the growling
the velvet the beads

the way she closed her eyes
her body shaking
the way
she held the mic

up to her mouth
and screamed
that scream

taking us up
bringing us down

Geri Digiorno

Margarete

we were inseparable in instant sister ship
you a lowdown big mama singer of ragtime
hands on hips cheeks blushed red lips
cocking your head to one side smiling
a deep throaty voice growling out each song
as incandescent beads and baubles moved you
and me your audience

until you dropped me for rosie
the hot dog queen
and called me up to tell me
how much a better friend she was
than I had been

Geri Digiorno

How Can We Ever Forget

the image of the pelicans
sitting weighted down with oil
unable to move

only a small percentage will survive

the image of a beautiful dragonfly
it's long marked tail and iridescent wings
sitting stuck in the oil
it's life stopped

how can we ever forget

Michael Castro

Giveaway

Indians in Forest Park
by the fake totem poles
in the southwest hills above the golf course & the zoo.
Tonight is a giveaway
to celebrate the breaking of a three month camp.
A ceremony
marking the ending of a vigil
in support of one Leonard Peltier
jailed ten years now, railroaded behind FBI lies
tracking "murder most foul."
So it goes.
A summer prayer vigil on the stony steps
of the United States Court of Appeals, 7th District,
in downtown St. Louis,
within whose interior noosphere
judges listlessly debate
whether or not to hear
recantations, admissions, legal improprieties, the accumulated
evidence of gross government misconduct, a federal frame-up.
The jailings of Crazy Horse, Sitting Bull,
their subsequent assassinations,
woven in the jagged blanket pattern
these neo-tribal people peek out of
& bear witness to.

     A vigil culminating in these
sweet September sundown breezes
dance of light & shadow
between shimmering leaves.

An old story.
A leader, one loved & respected by the people,

one whose existence touched the soul, a young man
described as "beautiful," & "strong,"
offering resistance,
offering spirit to matter,
taken away, clanged behind bars,
stored on the shelf
of a stacked system.

Still
a stirring, another
expression somewhere, miles away,
here, St. Louis, this stew
the people make to nourish each other,
raising smoke to the whispy clouds.
Golfers are gone.
Rainbow people are gone.
A spirit remains.
The park is alive.

Fragrances of coffee & potluck
wind round noses up to the sky.
Indians mixing easily in these hills
with local folk who've answered their call,
offering tonight thanks to this community
of beings for its support, for responding to the drum,
pulse of ailing Mother Earth—
gifts of thanks to friends & relatives,
outsiders, fools, poets, seekers
of some point or, even better,
some circular condition
where inside meets out
where nature is a smile or a spear
of saxifrage breaking through concrete.
Thanks for your concern.
Thanks for being connected.

Van, an anthropologist, adjusts the sound system;
Vicki, the pow-wow dancer, gravitates toward the drum;

graybeard Jim sips coffee from styrofoam cup; he's walked
this park for decades—the wino fifties, the caddying years,
the cleansing acid era digging trees,
the community organizer cogitation strolls, & now—
Buddha-bellied, hair severely cut, "realigning associations"
as urban zen sage;
John the guitar player flits about the scene like a firefly
buzzing his immanently silent music,
the burnt out case of his mute
instrument, as always, in hand;
& bug-eyed Bruce appears, less giddy than usual
having spent the past week in the workhouse
for refusal to pay parking tickets; proclaimed to judge,
"You sir, are a cad. . ."
Craggy Sam, his hair a wild gray bush,
& sister Becky, ballasted by shopping bags,
intense in hungry ghostly hover round the table—they've spent
years developing the art form of free dining at cultural events,
foraging free food & fellowship & thought, cookies for
consciousness
       their own circuit, body & spirit at once nourished—
at home everywhere, by choice,
homeless...

Raul Salinas moderates
the giveaway:
"in appreciation," he says, "to those who kept the camp going,
the fires lit. . .
"Anna Judson of the Indian Center, here every day,
seeing that no one went hungry. . .
"John the Mechanic, who kept our vehicles well. . .
"Crow, who worked on Security.
Where are you Crow? Crow? . .

The names,
the people, the givers,
come up & receive their gifts

& return.

The circle connects.
The giving goes on.

"Floyd Westerman. Where's Floyd?"
Our singer. . .
Floyd's in the sweat lodge
set up down by the creek
unnoticed by park patrons all these years.
"Our singer's down by the water, sweating, getting clean. . ."

Byron Clemens, fresh from interviewing Peltier
at Leavenworth, lumbers up. What amazed Clemens
was, that after all these years of unjust incarceration,
mostly in solitary, there was no bitterness in the man.
He greeted me, a white man, a total stranger, a journalist,
with the biggest, most soul-filled smile. . .

Salinas calls up lanky Steve Ribidoux, twin braids dangling
down to his waist, to talk about Leonard's case.
Ribidoux says, "Leonard's case relates to what's happening
at Big Mountain, where the government picks off Indians
& the energy companies flap over the land like buzzards. . .
says, "it relates to Wounded Knee, where the machine gun
was introduced to combat the Ghost Dance. . ."
says, "it relates to the secret war introduced in our lifetime . ." says,
"it relates to what's happening to Mother Earth. . .

we are concerned for all of these reasons. . .
"we are concerned because
the wrong man is behind bars for murder. . ."

Giving away gifts,
Iron-gray pigtailed Salinas,
slight of build but wiry tough,
whose smack poetry I'd copped to

weeks earlier at the Sunshine Inn,
looks clear here behind Gandhian glasses.
Beyond prison blues, feet fat with blisters,

at peace—this warrior, returned
from the most recent struggle, a demonstration
of solidarity, the long march of return from Leavenworth
the hundreds of miles from the former military outpost now
federal pen, where Leonard, mysteriously,
    is going blind

    before the very eyes
    of Soviet doctors & observers; his words, spirit, borne
by Salinas across the state of Missouri, misery, the sick
    liver near the American heart,
    all the organs
    pumping out sour notes,
back to this archway, this ancient city of mounds
where three rivers meet, this world's fair
site where Geronimo signed autographs,
back to the neo-Roman facades of the Federal Courthouse
where judgment is due at some imminent but unspecified date,
back to the hills of Forest Park
above the golf course & the zoo, precisely
here, back
Salinas beams under the cool moon.

Mary Bolton says, "I haven't been to anything like this in years.
It makes me remember who I am."

As the drummers begin
we all join hands,
& form a human circle;
dance with light &
    heavy deliberation,
one,
    with each other,
with Leonard
whom most of us

    have never seen,
chanting wordless sounds
    from a part of the self
    with no name,

a fluttering vibration
    unseen sundown songbirds join.

Paternal sunlight setting,
    maternal
half moon on the rise,
a delicate balance,
this moment
we are alive.

*

Months later,
the judges deny the appeal.

Peltier remains behind bars.
In Missouri
Monsanto researches terminator gene technology,
seeds that grow plants that won't grow seeds,
the great vision of corporate monopoly on food-stuff & life.
On the rez
Power Companies
strip mine, raping the earth,
& leaving it desolate—
bury their contaminated waste here
beneath indigenous soil.

They buried Sitting Bull.
Appeal denied.
They buried Crazy Horse.
Appeal denied.
Buffalo sentenced to extinction.
Appeal denied.
They mowed down the Ghost Dancers with gatling guns

& buried them in a mass grave.
Appeal denied.
Life, power, unity.

Appeal denied.

Michael Castro

Them

I am an endangered species
yet I am human
& I am free
living in eternity

but also from birth
on this planet earth
in the system
of Them

Them been here
since the beginning of fear
Them dragged me wailing from the womb
Them'll bury me silent in the tomb

Them granted curiosity
& planted a forbidden tree
Them's tricky, full of mystery
Them writes the book of history

Them is nameless, Them is free
Shameless as authority
Them's blameless in non-entity
The same whatever century

Them calls me woman, calls me man
Them tells me what I can't & can
Them calls me nigger, calls me jew
Them's neat as a nazi, twisted as a screw

Them etches furrows in my head
& drives me from my marriage bed
to walk the furrowed path Them paved

lonely, weary, to the grave

Them draws me close
then rends me apart
Them aches my head
Them breaks my heart

Them makes me work
& sweat & sigh
Them brings me down
Them gets me high

Them pits me against
my sister & brother
(not to mention
my earthen mother)

Them runs amok
Them calls for order
Them signs the deed
Them lines the border

Them is rich
so I stay poor
Them says 'love'
when Them means 'war'

Them is the enemy
of all mankind
Them hides somewhere
 in my mind

Them smashes the atom
The end is near
Soon Them or Us
must disappear

Susan Deer Cloud

Ode to O Holy Nights in Liberty, New York

Discharged from Air Force, your poet cousin
returned home. You ran away from University
to rejoin the Universe. Kent State shootings were past,
Vietnam War wasn't. Daisies the Flower Children planted
in gun barrels failed to seed peace. You had chanted
"1 2 3 4, we don't want your fuckin' war," dodging
tear gas on D.C. streets instead of smelling the Catskill roses.
You got a job typing for Liberty Community Action Center,
signed letters to Representative Hamilton Fish, Jr.—
Peace & Love, Love & Kisses or RED POWER.
Your cousin and trickster you rented an apartment
above Goody's Bar & Grill, ninety bucks a month—split
rent, bought some youthful freedom. He said "cool"
to your occupying the large front room with high
windows laced by wood diamonds across upper panes.
You grinned "groovy," bought a waterbed and gold
silk India spread embroidered with peacocks.
That bed got pretty damned cold in colder weather,
dreamed other cocks would be its heating element.
Your cousin and you tossed socks and underwear
in upside down wampum purple umbrella dangling
from ceiling lamp cord, first sight to greet people
when they blew in through the open door.
Back then, visitors appeared like sweet winds—
but in the 21st century this gets harder to explain.
You rescued a black kitten with panther eyes
from the alleyway, named her "Cocaine"
after a Dave Van Ronk song. You and your cousin
dined on berries, tamari-splashed brown rice,
Brie on baguettes, washed simplicity down
with peppermint tea—every meal a picnic
brightening your bare floor. You felt so Rimbaud,
so Baudelaire. You washed tea down with Bordeaux

the tint of garnets. Neon sign under windows blinked on
and off until sunrise, flashed scarlet electrons over walls,
ceiling, fragile skins of anyone who graced your room.
Friends sat in a tribal circle and didn't "Bogart that joint."
Ike shot smack up in windowless bathroom, skin-
popped a few other hungering freaks. Jimmy,
cousin's oldest friend, died last year of Hep-C.
"Closer to me than my own brothers," your cousin's
voice squeezed through a thousand miles of phone wire.
We didn't cry. We had gotten used to it.
You listened to silence, remembering
two Indian boys "playing Indian"
during the McCarthy years. Tommy died
of Aids in San Francisco, where he retreated
to escape small town hatred. After 9/11
Ike became a right wing flag waver, only thing
left for him to wave. You missed the decade
when he was nodding off. Sammy, paralyzed
in a teenage diving accident, died in 1975
from lung failure. But in 1971 Liberty, long-haired
men bore his wheelchair up sagging stairs, parked him
like a king under that poster you found one rainy dawn
in a muddy gutter: WAR IS NOT HEALTHY
FOR CHILDREN AND OTHER LIVING THINGS.
When Sammy dropped acid, he believed he danced.
A paraplegic dancing on Owsley Orange Sunshine—
Man, that to us was more fuckin' beautiful
than Jesus walking on the sparkling waters.
Next, Jimmy would hallucinate into a shaman
with trickster hair black as Raven's feathers,
rainbows flickering in its flying strands.
The hippie women smiled mellow yellow
in granny dresses flowering down to
patchouli-anointed feet which kicked away
all shoes, boots and any bra-burner bullshit
yelling "Men are sexist pigs!" "Just most
of you are," they'd toke and joke, joyfully
braless from the time they sprouted tits.
"Burn what bra?" Off and on

like the nights' neon, everybody bounced
and balled on the sloshing waterbed.
Except Sammy, of course, who was dancing
with the peacock sun. He had a crush
on green-eyed Lucy who slashed her artist's
wrists when Disco discolored life to polyester.
We played flutes, guitars, blues harps.
Your cousin, spouting naked poetry,
and flapping his skinny arms,

became a rebirth of Thunderbird.
We sang, poetry
and flapping his skinny arm giggled madly, couldn't stop
laughing our rapture and absurdity.
Nor did we suspect in Liberty's holy red light
that made every lover look Indian—
an American winter was descending
to bury us, little by little,
in big white lies.

Susan Deer Cloud

Sunday School

"I'll call you every week," you promise, voice of reunion diving
towards my voice inside telephone wire-strung out mystery
bordering New York Route 17, cosmic umbilical cord
connecting your Manhattan to my upstate Indian territory.

Your words, old friend ~ wine-drenched poetry, myhrr-scented
Jewish prophet cries ~ flash me back like a rainbow trout
bursting through water into air, cracking surfaces of submerged
worlds, snagging sunlight with its wet body's speckled twisting
before splashing down into forgetting depths. Your words

flash me back to 1970-secret invasion of Cambodia,
student uprisings, soldiers still children murdering other children
on Kent State's chemically treated lawns. Your words flash me back
to late June when you visited me in Catskill Mountains ~ Onteora ~

bearing the gift of your mescaline-induced madness, your Holy Land
eyes, blue as sky, green as earth, elusive as quicksilver.

And there I guided you to where we could skinny-dip in Indian-named
Willowemoc, solitary river spot separated by far-flung meadows
from all roads, you and me slow-motion-moving through tall grasses
down to stony shore, ripping off clothes, stripping off strobe-light
insanities of 1960's Vietnam War, War protests, assassinations,
drug-induced crying ~ screaming ~ for a vision.

There we entered, hand-in-hand, into sacred Willowemoc ~
mountain laurel spilling across cliffs, summer sun water spiders

of light spinning on rapids—until our naked flesh grew innocent, again,
in the river's cold baptism, you lifting me with your arms, dear friend,

73

kissing, kissing my eyes shut. Eyes opening ~ on river edge, eyeing us,
my former Sunday School class ~ class I taught

because my little sister was in it ~ because I wished her to learn
about the true Christ. Who in church remembered the tender, loving
Jew who talked peace/love poetry—long-haired and tribal the way
we Indians were before centuries of holocaust-hate? Friend
of Heaven-and-Earth eyes, that day we offered up our bodies freely,
so freely I knew my Sunday School children with amazed faces

for the first time beheld Christ with his Dearly Beloved, you
with your Mohawk Magdalene. "I'll call," you promise,
baptisms of words like river water flowing peacefully through
sunlit wire, swirling along Indian trails lost beneath hard highway.
Telephone powwow ~ O tender, O broken, brother calling
me after too many crucified years.

Sherry Pasquarello

peace and patchouli

we became without becoming
were before we

knew
we knew we were

new yet old as time
it was a time

our time

of peace and patchouli
power to the people

and to the young
that we were

joy to the world
that we were becoming

that almost became til

our time passed us
faster than we could run

now we were but
are

again

slow but steady
wise enough

to become again
our time.

Sherry Pasquarello

a poetry tale

little wanna be

"and where do your ideas come from
the words for your little POEMS?"

with the tone of voice only
the over educated can pull off

subtle
but not

he smiled down from his lofty height

waiting for little wanna be
to scurry away
like a bug when a rocks been kicked over

"where?"
little wanna be looked up
eyes wide with a smile
that wasn't
a smile only the littles can pull off

and said

"don't know." cause
little wanna, she knew right then
that he wasn't
and she was

keeping the answer to herself.

Sherry Pasquarello

river rocks

knife edged waves
steel grey sharpness
slicing away at the river rocks.
cold raw silver skied day
you can see them
packed tight
under the bridges of the three rivers.
dirty blankets
stained cardboard
muted colors
dulled hopes endure.
eyes as hard as the wet stones
staying while the river flows
away.

Sherry Pasquarello

love stinks

there's an old rock song with that title
can't fucking remember who sang it
doesn't much matter
I know the words by heart
by heart, HA!
It was a selection on the jukebox where I hang
me and a friend, we used to play it a couple of times
ah hell, more than a couple. every friday and saturday night.
We'd sing love"sucks" instead of stinks
suck being shouted
his girl tending bar didn't like that
we did.
he married her
needed a steady income.
love sucks

Joy Leftow

Welfare's Still A Bitch

Back in the day I burned loquacious at welfare's fair hearings
But soon I learned that when you went to your worker you only
speak when you're spoken to Everything will be held against you
 And twice more if you're white
You'll be accountable for every damn penny you didn't spend
How dare you go to Columbia University on our money
You'll see white bitch hoe
Now I'm at the welfare center again
I'm still the only white one there
thank god it's not for me I wait here
I watch as everyone demands entitlements
They have their appointments they'll not leave with disappointment
The brothers and sisters and me we see others get special treatment
waiting on names and numbers to be called
Liars they say first come first served but everything seems stalled
I want mine and I want it now - Latinos and Blacks uprising.
The guards are watchful but do nothing
Those who yell loudest—their workers came out and usher them
through glass doors to get what's theirs
they come back smiling
After that it didn't quiet down till the room emptied out
After they all got what was coming to them
I wish it had been like that for me
I fought at so many fair hearings
To get my claims accepted back in the day
Each time I recertified they cut my food stamps to zero
If you're white you get less
if you're Jewish it's double less because you know all those jews
are rich they don't come from any Warsaw ghettos and it's a damn
lie any of them were killed in any fucking holocaust
those kikes are Fucking Christ killers is what they are
heard it all my life

A voice inside my head
Each way I turn
Sometimes I forget who I am

And it all comes rushing home like a river overflowing with leaves
        silt memories
Someone will bring it home to me no matter how long I live

Ladies and Gentlemen: we've gone back in time to the 60's—
prejudice crackles like fire in the air.

We need to get our heads turned back to the streets to take back
what's rightfully ours

We need we need we need—medical care money a place to live
        and survive
So sad - right back at you with the blues tonight

Joy Leftow

Billie's Dog Rescue Blues: Bluetry – #8

Billie's blues on my mind tonight
I've morphed into Billie singing my blues to her blues we are one
Your protestations sink into my instrumentals
Everything's easy to get on the Internet; you can get whatever you want to.

I'm a fool to want you, for heaven's sake why am I in love, here's a chance fall in love.

I race up the stairs to face closing doors #1 train, elevated. A second too late. For God's sake, my breath jagged, voice barely whispers on exhale. A golden red-nosed puppy stands before me, jumps on the bench next to DubbleX. Eye to eye, dilemmas & sadness everywhere.

DubbleX says forget the train roars up the watches drama ensues. The dog shaking, wet & wary furry pretty fur seeking solace and warmth. Train pulls in dog runs for the open doors, crevice between the platform & train. I see him go under. I grab him by the flesh on his neck; pull him away from the closing door. Another moment stolen from death. The pup whines, returns to the bench. My heart skips a Billie holiday beat.

This revolution will not be televised it will not put the shine back on your teeth. How bout the belt from my bag - I greedily grab it. Pup accepts collar attempts to climb into my arms again.

Kneel down Johnny, heel, his haunches pressed to my thighs, crouched beside him, clinches the blended holiness of earth and sky. Pressed to my chest, his tongue sweeps my neck. Paws bleeding raw — ice & sleet on the pavement.
Let's agree to be in love like a melody. Wet white snow falling huge flakes drop on my face. I can't go where I want to.

Money you've got lots of friends crowding right your door,
but when you're gone and nothing's left, they don't come round no more.

I want to go back when things were changing. Now things are suspended or turning backwards. I don't understand. Race for faith, blood bath, Kent State massacre, more prejudice now then before.

Baby pit follows me whining. I bend to examine torn ragged paws, bloodied from standing in deep salted snow, blizzards outside the station. He covers me with kisses, dutifully remains still a second then jumps on my chest. Here, boy, Here. I crouch down he throws himself in my arms shaking.

Downstairs the token booth clerk says cops are on their way. My heart booms, a gut reaction, not my future. I hold red nose with my make shift collar. He pulls me he's strong, his attention span like a child's eye caught by mischief, his shaking visible to everyone. Cops show up, act afraid even when they see him sucking my face. The sgt arrives he doesn't know what to do. Finally a cage from the station arrives. I take charge, tell them how to put him in there away from my caring arms.

I'm a fool to want you. A red nosed pit bull with tail & ears intact. Will they find a home for him? My heart sings collateral let freedom ring, life on a hinge.

David Wiseman

Caught Jesus Smoking Weed

A spark snapped into flame,
the water gurgled,
and from within a cloud
He spoke.

Bade us all to sit at His feet,
because the couch was occupied
by the three of Him.

Laughed at His own joke
pulled a pizza from thin air.
It figures that He would like
anchovies.

He was chronically kind,
and in His kindness
passed around all that He had.

Bade us all fare well
and took His leave
but we are all sure
He'll be back,
and we'll be right here.

David Wiseman

On Mapping a Slave Cemetery

Chasing a real estate deal, we tromped through the woods,
batting in vain at left-over spider webs that stuck to our faces
and glued specks of digested bugs into our hair.
We carried a bundle of small pink flags and a hundred-foot tape measure.
Last November's leaves crashed under our feet so loud we could
hear no other sound.
We follow a small creek that seemed to laugh at our work.

Someone must have known these graves were here, such digging
takes much work.
They would be easy to overlook, so modest in these resurrected woods
vague depressions littered with years, forgotten by sight, deprived of
even the rattling sound
of leaves and cracking limbs that rot and dissolve into the ground,
Neglected bones, forgotten faces.
Like a suture scar, the stones, one at the head, one at the foot. Five
paces measure
the separation of each stitch in this ragged streak . A poison vine
snakes through, covered in woody hair.

We are three, me, my father, and his business partner. Three
divorces between us have greyed our hair.
Whiskey-stained brains, anger-smudged faces, all that brightens this
day is the bleach of work.
Plans, and deals that fill the gaps as jagged stones fill a glass jar,
incompletely and tense. Measure
them wrong and the shattering will foul the room with rough and
bleeding words. In these quiet woods
we can put that risk away and search for graves unnamed and
remark how each one faces
the same direction, east, toward the morning sun, waiting for
resurrection's trumpet to sound.

Three graves make the first row, six little pink flags, fifteen feet, ten inches, call it sixteen. The sound
of a train rattles the air. No one lying in this ground ever heard a locomotive before his hair
was eaten by worms and time. "Him", maybe there are women in this ground too. Their faces,
what did they look like? We cannot know. The fields and barns too are gone where they did their work.

Twenty-nine feet, let's make it thirty. We want to give them space to rest in these woods.
One grave, off by itself, separated for some reason in space; bonded by time. We must re- measure.

The graveyard grows, taking in a hemlock with soft needles. Its height and girth measure
time better than any calendar, or watch, or even the bones of man. Strange as it may sound
it feels like we have found some treasure in these Virginia woods; a record of lives and deaths, of how even the church yard eternity was denied by the kink of hair
and the tint of skin. Their graves we will forever mark on maps, maybe some good comes of this work,
beyond money, beyond the satisfaction of the deal. We cannot give back their names or faces,

but someone now knows they are here. To die and have even his grave forgotten, a fate every man faces
perhaps this mapping restores something stolen. Perhaps it eases the lingering guilt by a small measure,
or hands a fraction of satisfaction to our own lives, something greater than this survey work.
Maybe, though, we are just hiding here in the spring, in this cool hollow, off a twisty road with the sound
of birds. Our task is clear, draw a shape on a map. No lawyers, paperwork, or angry women in our hair.
This is why men go into the woods.

We would sell these woods, and the graves in them. Could we tell them to their faces
that even in death they are property? It will grey our hair, the answer. We may measure
ourselves against the past, but the sound of shovels digging will work its way to our ears.

David Wiseman

Transition and Memory

At the very moment the sun snaps from blanket to welding rod,

a pelican cruises the sky over the Neutral Ground and
bronze Ignatius tolerates
one more photograph.

At the very moment an airplane
moves from small graceful sky
to dinosaur lumbering land,

a child staring out the window
of an apartment sees something
she will never forget.

At the very moment an explosion
moves the building
into rubble,
an old man's face rises with moonlight glow
when he flips a book
to a particular page.
At the very moment afternoon leans into clear
purple and the first bat
sorties through the air,
a wife finds a fading card in the back
of a drawer and rides
that motorcycle once more.
As the television high on the wall flashes
from the bright games to the podium
men in dark suits,

the pock-faced man with scrambled eggs
on the bill of his cap growls
through discount cigarette smoke
"Boy, you don't know shit."

Teck Loh

Afterthoughts

Prologue:

The world is divided into two parts: the First World and the Third. Countries in the First World, which are to be found in North America and Europe, appreciate the values of intelligence, creativity and freedom. Although far from being utopias, conditions in First World countries are considered to be bearable and even nurturing for humans.

The Third World is a collection of prison dimensions. Examples include Singapore, Burma and North Korea. Humans who have the misfortune to be born in the Third World (like myself) are destined to live out their miserable existence as prisoners subjected to the rulership of the Third World Lords and their minions. Intelligence and creativity are considered to be vices and unhealthy in the Third World (unless you are a Lord).

Occasionally, denizens of the Third World do visit the First World. There, they may gain valuable insights and learn what it is like to be free. Those are the unfortunate ones, for while they may be granted temporary respites from the Third World, they are still unable to live out their lives in the First World. What is worse than having to live as a prisoner in the Third World is having to live as a prisoner with the knowledge that things could be different.

Mike has left the city.

I spent the day of his arrival, the 4th of October, in anticipation. I had to work at the mall that day and couldn't pick him up at the train station. Even as I stood under the bright artificial lights of the mall, looking at the throngs of my fellow prisoners going about their last minute Sunday shopping, in my own prison that is so far removed from the First World, I couldn't help but remember scenes from a past life. A past life in the First World that included Mike, amongst other citizens of the First World who taught me what I knew now about freedom: their birthright as First Worlders.

Yet whatever eagerness I might have felt had been dulled by a sense of resignation to my fate; a depressive resignation caused by years of captivity without any hope of release. So it was with a quiet anticipation that I awaited the end of my shift when I would receive a call from Mike. It was the sort of calm anticipation a prisoner serving a life sentence might have at the thought of having a dear friend visit; a short respite from the dull and permanent drudgery of captivity.

His visit was most welcomed. It came at a time when my depression, after years of failure to break free from Singapore, has reached an all time low. I have already descended past the melodramatic gloom-and-doom phase into the calm rapids of resignation-to-my-fate. I thought I would have to live out the rest of my life in Singapore without ever seeing the First World again.

Then Mike hopped along for a short visit. Mike. A First Worlder. In my prison dimension (Singapore). It felt good and surreal at the same time.

It was good because having a First Worlder here was as if a ray of hope was allowed to filter through the dark barriers of my prison, and through the crack left by its passing, I could glimpse the splendor of the First World that is denied me.

At the park we visited, I mentally superimposed bits of Golden Gate park over the one in my prison and I tried hard to reach out with my mind, as if I visualized hard enough I could actually touch a real piece of Golden Gate Park using Mike as a conduit. As we sat down at my table for dinner, I remembered scenes from the Zeit Geist, a bikers pub in San Francisco, where we too shared a meal together.

Zeit Geist seemed so far away, in another time and another place. Yet at the same time, with Mike sitting just right across the table from me, it seemed so close. As if just by merely concentrating, I could hear the background din of loud music and drunken cheer and feel the cool San Franciscan breeze sweep away the stagnant humidity of my prison.

It was surreal because Singapore is to me what Kryptonite is to Superman, and yet Mike could walk around with impunity; the oppressive vibes rolling off him as water off a duck's back. And he could leave. The Third World is no place for a First Worlder. Mike could escape to his haven in the First World, but I can't. So our relationship, my relationship with other First Worlders in fact, is ... strange. I have long accepted that we are not so unequal in terms of strength and intellect, and yet even the weakest First Worlder possesses powers beyond my wildest imagination: they can enter and leave my prison as they will. The barriers surrounding Singapore (nationality, family, poverty and education) are as real as concrete walls to me, yet they pose no more hindrance to the First Worlders than a slab of butter would to a hot knife.

As I watched Mike depart through the departure gate, I wondered when I will be granted another respite from the monotony of my captivity; when I will be granted another vision from the First World.

Teck Loh

Americanism

Recent events in my life have prompted me to think about my identity. My frequent trips to the USA and my attempts to bring a little "America" into my life have faced opposition from friends and family alike. They feel that sensible and conservative Asians should not be gallivanting around with "decadent" western ideas. It seems disloyal for me to adopt ways native to a foreign country.

When I visited the city of San Francisco, my mind was blown away by the revelations I received. Political and social freedoms do not lead to the erosion of societal values or the destruction of businesses! All my life, I believed otherwise. Until I witnessed the responsible and empowered citizenry of San Francisco speaking their minds (in public!) and embarking on their missions to make the world a better place without once causing the mythical "collateral damage" the propagandists so enjoy spinning about.

I think it is simplistic to define a country as just a place: a patch of soil and rocks. What exactly is Singapore? What is America? America is more than just a place. It is also a set of ideals. When I say I am American, it means I believe in the dignity of human beings. It means that I believe in freedom. It means I believe in the Constitution designed to protect values every human being holds dear. It is unfair and absurd to tell me that I should not believe in these values simply because I was born in another country. I feel like a kid who is being punished for something he did not do.

However, different people have different "Americas".

It came to pass that a former classmate of mine visited San Francisco just like I did. And had a radically different experience, unlike the Renaissance awakening that I had. During a class reunion, he coldly informed me that San Francisco was a "dangerous city" populated by street bums who congregated in "threatening numbers" at public venues. He was at UN Plaza one evening, and having witnessed Food Not Bombs activists doling out food to the destitute, completely missed the message of selfless sacrifice and compassion for one's fellow human beings.

To be fair, he's not a snob. The better dressed college students from UC Berkeley came under his fire as well. The petition drives organized on campus to protest against various social injustices were lambasted as "threatening to the fabric of society", and more importantly, "not good for their studies".

Some people manage to move their bodies around, but their minds never take a single step out of their heads.

Robert Priest

You Were There

You were there
When the stars fell down
And burned my eyes

When the thirst was at its worst
You stayed without water
To be with me

You were there
When I was nowhere
You walked beside me in the abyss
And when I stood impoverished
With nothing to declare
You were there

I felt it in your touch
I felt it in your care

There was never a time
When I was unaware

of your presence
your essence

Every place I left
You left with me
And when I got anywhere
It was like you had preceded me
It was like you had always been there
awaiting my arrival.

Robert Priest

V

Churchill flashed his famous V sign
it wasn't for victory
as everyone says
it was for vagina
for Churchill knew
what I know
that there is still not enough praise

for the lining of the vagina
he knew that if anything is a miracle
that the relation between the inside of the vagina
and the outside of the penis
is a miracle

Nixon knew this too
even as he resigned
even as he turned to face the music of his own destiny
he flashed that last peace sign "V"
but my friends
it was not a peace sign
it was Nixon's way of saying
that the inside of the vagina
is as numinous as it gets

this secret is well known
the lining of the vagina
the shape of the vagina
is a sign
without which not a single

holy thing may be written

DubbleX

The People's Republic of America

The dictator knows whom I call and who calls me
The dictator knows where I go and whom I see
The dictator knows the sites I surf ~ the emails I send
The text messages I receive
They know all my bank accounts and social security numbers and fake ID's
They know my race age and sexual orientation
They know my tribal nation
Political affiliation and activist organization
I have been filmed and photographed too many times to mention
filed and data based placed
Tracked by satellites
Followed by GPS OnStar hooked to my car
The dictator censors the news so I only hear the untruth
Their propaganda campaign distorts perceptions
Protection from terrorists
Protect me from dictatorships
As my civil liberties have been stripped
Innocent citizens detained tortured and whipped
Illegal wars to over throw and take more
The Geneva Convention is something that's not mentioned
Extraordinary Rendition covert political CIA missions
My fellow Americans your democracy has been hijacked
Not by terrorist
But the Patriot Act
Read the facts
No search warrants
Unlimited wire taps
cast your vote note write it in quotes
they change the name
political scapegoats
promote their result
the so called cleansing of the voting roles

Blacks are bounced falsely accused criminals on parole
Government officials on company payrolls
The dictator commits crimes without consequence trails or sentence
Hiding behind the lines of its classified access denied no further reply
as another war looms and more innocent die.
They put a microchip in my fingertip
Tattooed a serial number on the back of my neck
They want me to believe land of the free home of the brave
Didn't they kill millions of Native Americans and made my ancestors slaves

DubbleX

2 for 1

gonna sell sell sell sell = sell it
you need to smell better
look better
love better
have a bigger cock
have your period better
cramp better
dress better
eat what we say
when we say
how we say
where we say
got 2 be a clone but think you're an original rebel
buy all the worthless junk that will break down in a month
we've got the ugliest clothes that you've got to have
believe all the lies
shave your legs better
brush your teeth with a laser
change your brown eyes to original orange
your eyebrows are out of style
shave your head
now grow it back
dye it
curl it
burn it
weave it
deceive it
achieve it
nothing more then buying
from infomercials
commercials
click that internet ad
latest fade

junk mail
spam
all creating
forming
and deforming
who I was
and who I am
scram
want out of this jam
don't need your new version of Windows
mutilation of a nation
a world and generation
fall prey to the hype
this advertising life
only to find
they want more
ads fly across the sky
sketched in the sand
implanted in your brain
dial a lawyer
phone a friend
liposuc the fat from your gut
new pair of breasts on your flat chest
WiFi and HD
4G phones in your hand
you can talk
surf
fuck
shit
dance
spit
do a split
while you drive your high polluting
gas chugging
SUV up the freeway
70 miles an hour
Reading each billboard sign
For the next high tech design
Not realizing that you done gone lost your mind

Mikel K. Poet

Has Anybody Seen Bob Dylan?

Has anybody seen Bob Dylan?
I heard that he was down on Rodeo Drive.

Has anybody seen Bob Dylan?
Does he know that there is a war in Iraq?

Has anybody seen Bob Dylan,
since he used social protest
to make a name for himself;

Zimmerman sure knew how
to sell c.d.'s?

Has anybody seen Bob Dylan?
I sure hope that I'm wrong in this song,

but I heard that Bob Dylan
is primarily counting benjamins
in Beverly Hills.

Has anybody seen Bob Dylan?
Has anybody seen Bob Dylan?

Mikel K Poet

What's the Solution to War?

What's the solution to war?
We should send old men and old women
to war, let them kill themselves off
in the name of bigger cars and better
air conditioning.

Let the congressmen and the kings,
the presidents and the heads of state
pull out guns and knives and battle
to the death.
Why should my son or daughter fight
for you, you fucking cowards, you killers,
you creeps.

You hide behind your hallow halls,
you hide behind your laws that money buys.

I want you out in the open
looking down the barrel of a gun,
see what my son would see,

before he pulled the trigger,
a man just like himself,
scared just like himself,
put there just like himself
by a man like you.

The blood that spills
the guts that pour
should be yours, Mr. President.

The guts that pour,
the blood that spills

should be yours, Speaker of the House.

The brains that splat,
the guts that pour,
the blood that spills
should be yours, Senator.

Teenagers should not be killing teenagers,
they should be studying math.
or tearing down an engine,
or hitchhiking through Europe.

War is not a game of chess.

The revolution will not be televised
at a five star restaurant

I'm so much a part of
the machine
that I will probably
never revolt against anything
more than the waiter who brings me
my steak cooked incorrectly.

Misty Serna

Into Freedom

Into Freedom
Into Peace
Into the New World we must embrace
Boldness to be different
Daring to be real
Showing others it is ok to feel
Together in love for all of mankind
Leaving hate and war behind
Oh the future i want to see
Into Freedom you and me....

Craig Murray

cnn

Fat ass and flip flops
She walks like a pigeon
TV dinner hips
And empty vessel eyes
Staring at painful orange
plastic dishes
The trash of summer

Artificial fuck monkeys

And dazzle headed kids
Jerk and yell and spit
In parody of being human

Nothing a punch in the head
Wouldn't fix

Shit music drones overhead
A replacement for a soul
A substitute for feeling

A discount store world

of bullshit and vagaries
I hate them all
Call in the clowns

The things of life
A life of things
Bills and calls
And credit card junkies

Oprahs desperate collection
Of non functional
Fuckwads

The radio sprays
Precanned shit across
The room
Teenage egos and
Plastic sounds
Emptiness
For a buck

There is no feeling anymore
No one feels
Anything of substance
Useless shit

And pretend correct Anger
replace thought

march in a protest
if its fashionable
hate the haters
and burn their fucking

churches down
as long as cnn says so

fuck you ted
a billion dollars

for spreading the misery
of the planet
twenty four
hour a day angst
it's a planetary
suicide watch

tell me something I don't know

Craig Murray

Needs

What do you want
Wandering lost

 And empty
Filling your life
With bags of crap
Stuffing the un needed
Into the unfulfilled
We slave for image
And image is ignored
A purchased face
Of plastic trash
Just stop
Just try
Scream and throw
The shit to the ground
Look at it
Look at what you want
Is it all you hoped
It would be
Senseless noises
And idiot motions
Detract from the simplicity
Of a blade of grass
Crush it
Buy it
Save it
Invest it
Fuck it

Craig Murray

The Bar

Sliding desperately
to the cloying grasp
of middle aged mediocrity
she still claws futilely
to the appearances
and attitude of
womanhood.

The young girl
at the end of the bar smiles,

her face a mask
of saccharine sweetness
and artificial interest
in a world that races past her.

All she has is her youth;
all she has are
upturned breasts
and flawless skin
while still
the shadows of ages yet to come
superimpose themselves

like some grim shadow
of a world yet seen.

Craig Murray

I don't want to be like you

I don't want to be like you
I don't want
The shallow desires and
 Empty grasping needs
I want to create
I want to breath life
Into words
And watch them fly
I don't want suits and cars
And houses and titles

I don't want
Things
And stuff
And empty friends

I don't need
The shallow trappings
Of emptiness
And tv generated lust
I don't want
Bragging rights
And peroxide wives
I don't want to be like me

Craig Murray

Mediocrity

He desperately sought
to achieve mediocrity
And when he didn't
He was left standing alone
His face wrapped around the concepts
Of pointlessness
Like some discarded wrapper
Long since forgotten

He didn't come here on purpose

This wasn't his planned destination
Or final goal
Once as a child he had even dreamt
Of greatness
But the effort of design

Had never come
So still he stands
Failing even
To accomplish nothing
Was there a reason
Was there one thing he could point at
And mumble accusations

Or was it ten thousand
Cast aside decisions
And pointless movements
Far too young to give up
And far to old to be as he is
It's limbo for him
A drunken stagger
Through the rest of his days

Without even
The numbing effects of alcohol
 His drunkenness is internal
His stagger

Hidden
He'll keep going
There's nothing else to do
He doesn't know
Any better

Reflections

an excerpt from *Along the Templar Trail: Seven Million Steps for Peace*

— Brandon Wilson

"This is the way of peace — overcome evil with good, and falsehood with truth, and hatred with love."
— Peace Pilgrim

Cruising home at thirty thousand feet, in between the tiny bags of pretzels and constant interruptions, I had time to reflect on my wanderings. My introspection would continue long after my feet returned to their normal size. Although my journey of self-exploration felt gratifying, I hoped I'd accomplished more than finding personal peace and a communion with spirit. If anything, I hoped I was successful in sowing seeds of peace along a trail long used for war. Like a Johnny Appleseed, perhaps I'd planted a vision, while reminding folks they had non-violent options—one village, one person at a time.

Along the trail, I often imagined the possibilities if this same route were to become a pathway open to people of all cultures, faiths and nationalities to walk together; an international trail of peace. The simple act of walking together would nourish tolerance while dispelling fear, prejudice and hatred. Once people share a similar experience as intense as this one, they realize how much our hopes and fears are alike. Then again, everyday pilgrims would discover a tranquil sanctuary within, once they disconnect from an ever-more chaotic world. Returning home, more at peace and enlightened, it was only natural they would share this serenity and inspiration with families, friends and co-workers, as other *peregrinos* I know had done.

On the other hand, immersing yourself in other countries can be the best way to re-discover your own. I had five months of quiet, sometimes painful, sometimes inspired contemplation. Many days, I reflected on the root causes of our never-ending wars; a global imperative as we stand hip-deep in another quagmire.

Remembering back to those horrendous events of September 11th, 2001, with everyone seeking answers or revenge, we were promised the illusion of safety and freedom. All it took was war—and a pre-emptive one at that. Congress willingly complied, with few dissenting voices. The government would try not to disrupt our lives too much. As citizens, we were only asked to "keep shopping" and sacrifice a few liberties via the Orwellian-named Patriot Act—for our own security, of course.

However, war is never freedom; no more than black is ever white. The absence of war, peace, is freedom.

It's one thing to protect our homeland against aggressors, and I'd never advocate abandoning self-defense. But our invasion of Iraq was clearly not a case of self-preservation. Saddam Hussein had no links to Al-Qaeda, as we all know by now. Instead, we were sold a polished, pre-planned confrontation for "freedom" (and oil). It was a costly fabrication whose consequences will eat away at the fabric of our nation for generations to come, just as the debacle in Vietnam has done.

In today's world, it's far too easy to declare war, invade, and fire missiles at faceless targets below. In one sense, we can blame the media that present us with a sanitized view of death and destruction. Once the celebratory fireworks of "shock and awe" have passed, we see nothing of its aftermath and huge civilian casualties. After the devastation is complete, we leave our children and the rest of the world an even more precarious and pernicious legacy.

America deserves better.

Why is it the "Mission Accomplished" leaders of the world are often those who have never smelled the stench of gunpowder, gone deaf from the mortars' roar, or held a bloodied buddy in their arms? Let them first taste the grotesque horror of war, the sheer repulsion, and gut-wrenching fear—before sending another mother's naïve child to a needless, futile death on any foreign shore.

America deserves better.

I feel deeply sorry for the latest brave men and women who volunteered for our country, misled into believing they were protecting our homes. I mourn with my country for those thousands who will never see their sons and daughters again. I grieve over those tens of thousands whose scarred lives, and those of their loved ones, will never be the same because of the latest grand deception.

America deserves better.

If one thing, after this journey, I am certain most people of the world truly want and crave peace. If only their leaders will listen.

We can no longer continue on these paths of recklessness. The wanton destruction of nations' infrastructures—let alone their honor—only creates poverty, despair and more people left with nothing to lose. In the name of fighting "terrorism," we douse flames of poverty and resentment with oil. We create new generations of terrorists through our invasions, economic sanctions and wide-reaching actions. We bankrupt our own society by devoting the bulk of our national budget to the military industrial complex. At the same time, we dismantle freedoms and destroy the guiding principles on which our nation was founded.

If we are to eliminate the root cause of war and suffering, we need to assure the basic needs of our citizens at home are met, and in proxy, those of the world. As American president, general and military hero Dwight D. Eisenhower once said, "Every gun that is made, every warship launched, every rocket fired, signifies in the final sense a theft from those who hunger and are not fed, those who are cold and are not clothed." Today, our country feels that loss.

As someone traveling with his home upon his back for five months, I often thought of the less fortunate in our land of plenty. In my nightly search for a place to sleep, I remembered those thirty-six million Americans living in poverty. As I worried where my next meal would come from, I was reminded of the thirty-eight million of my countrymen who have trouble finding the money to keep food on their table—and the eighteen percent of American children who live in poverty. On my worst days, limping in pain, I sympathized with forty-five million Americans suffering because they have no health insurance to buy medicine. At those times when trucks zoomed past, throwing me into the ditch, I knew the fleeting transient nature of life and empathized with those who live day-to-day with violence. While nearly 4,000 soldiers have died in Iraq since our invasion, more than 65,000 people have been killed in America during the same four-year period. While walking cold and battered in the rain, I thought of those more than 3.5 million who would experience homelessness in America this year—25% of them employed—40% of them military veterans.

This is an American tragedy.

Fortunately, the brave are among us, awaiting a finer destiny, waiting to feel part of a greater, more noble cause. It's part of our nature and human heritage. It's one altruistic reason that some enlist in the military; to make life better, I believe—not to kill in the name of democracy.

As still free, conscious citizens of the world and true patriots, let us be the first to say, "Enough!" in one voice. It is time to channel those same selfless citizen efforts into social action, instead of destruction. Devote our abundance of resources to creating better lives. Eliminate poverty. House the homeless. Protect human rights. Care for the elderly. Protect our planet. Educate and teach our children tolerance. Rebuild our highways and infrastructure. Develop energy independence. Revitalize our cities and protect them from natural disasters. And wage war against devastating diseases.

It is time to win support for democracy through our generous deeds and social progress, instead of through aggression and violence.

It is time to never allow another politician to claim that improving the welfare of our citizenry and the state of the world is beyond our budget. For when it comes to war, America's wallet is always full—and always open.

These are national values that transcend bi-partisan politics. They are the ideals that helped our forefathers build a nation from wilderness. Once we set our mind to it, surely we can wage peace just as effectively as we've waged war. When there is hope and progress, when people can live their dreams, the need for international confrontation will wither on the vine. War profiteers, those peddlers of death, will disappear. Peace will prevail.

After seven million small steps, in my heart I know we can each make a difference. What progressive world movement has not begun small, even if by just one person with truth and determination; pilgrims committed to walking "roads less traveled."

We are all pilgrims, each on their own path, each with their own story to tell. Walking is only a first step, but one we each can take to discover the peace within. In that way, eventually, war will become unconscionable. Darkness will be dispelled with light—one person, one step at a time.

General Thein Sein Claps as Singapore Names an Orchid After Him

Seelan Palay

As preparations for the sham elections in Burma get into full swing, it is not difficult to notice similarities in electoral practices between the Burmese generals in uniform and Singapore's leaders in civilian clothes.

The Burmese regime is bending over backwards to stage the fraudulent elections while refusing to respect the results of the country's polls in 1990 that led to the landslide victory for the National League for Democracy (NLD).

Why reinvent the wheel, when what happened two decades ago remains unfulfilled? The same military that massacred thousands of innocent civilians, including Buddhist monks, is now pretending that everything is hunky dory.

It is an undeniable fact that the military regime holds close economic ties to Singapore—the top brass of the Burmese army are known to have parked their ill gotten millions in Singapore's banks, while they and their family members own properties in upmarket areas and their children go to top schools and drive flashy cars, flaunting their wealth to the envy of ordinary Singaporeans.

Burmese drug lords who are banned from entering the US freely come and go in Singapore and some even have offices in the posh commercial district along Shenton Way. It is no wonder that Singapore is the third largest investor in Burma, helping to prop up the pariah regime.

Singapore has even named a hybrid Orchid, its national flower, after the Burmese prime minister, General Thein Sein. Orchids in the same Singapore Botanical Gardens were previously named after Princess Diana and Nelson Mandela.

The similarities between Burma and Singapore do not stop there. The election process in Singapore is as opaque as it is in Naypyidaw, the new capital of the Burmese regime. Although Singapore claims to hold periodical elections to legitimise the rule of the People's Action Party (PAP), the exercise itself is highly questionable.

To start with, there is no independent elections commission. Only a department that comes under the Prime Minister's Office that decides on last minute boundary delineation, exorbitant deposits for candidates (presently $US9,900 but expected to be raised to $US11,000 in the next election), and other regular gerrymandering practices, including what is known as the Group Representation Constituencies (GRC).

This so-called electoral system has led to almost half of the seats in parliament being uncontested on Nomination Day. Presently, Singapore's "parliament" has 84 MPs, of which 82 are from Lee Kuan Yew's PAP. And that is "democratic elections" in Singapore for you!

The paradox of Singapore's elections is that the electorate, some of whom are nearing their 50s, have never voted in their entire lives. This so-called anomaly is glaring in Singapore, where voting is compulsory under the Parliamentary Elections Act.

With all these well entrenched undemocratic practices, it is not surprising to even a distant observer to understand how the ruling PAP has been in power since 1959.

What is worse is the irrefutable reality in Singapore that one man, by the name of Lee Kuan Yew, has been in power for the last 51 years. The octogenarian Lee, who is now 87 years old, calls himself Minister Mentor in the cabinet headed by his prime minster son, Lee Hsien Loong.

Compare this to the reality in Burma where the army generals have held sway since the 1962 coup, ousting the democratically elected government of U Nu. Even against this, Lee Kuan Yew's grip on power extends longer by three years, but he continues to claim that elections in his republic are based on the Westminster model of democracy.

Anyone who believes in democratic values could easily see that it is next to impossible to continue to have a one party dominated parliament in the name of freedom and democracy. Obviously the uniformed generals are under tutelage by the authoritarian regime in Singapore, clad in civilian clothes.

While the Burmese generals continue to not recognise the results of the 1990 elections, preparations are in full swing to hold yet another elections based on its 2008 constitution, aimed at hoodwinking the people. Singapore too is notorious for amending its constitution just before every general election to give a legal facade to what is clearly an illegitimate exercise.

The Burmese generals also appear to have been keen and obedient students to their teacher, Singapore. Burmese intelligence agents are known to visit on a routine basis to study the latest electronic eavesdropping gadgets for their surveillance of Burmese political dissidents, including the NLD leaders.

The recent announcement by NLD to boycott the army orchestrated sham elections is the right move. How can the elections be legitimate when NLD's leader, Daw Aung San Suu Kyi, remains under house arrest and barred from taking part? Singapore too, has a history of barring genuine opposition leaders who were daring enough to challenge, through constitutional means, the regime of Lee Kuan Yew.

Victims of Lee's political vendetta include prominent figures such as the late J B Jeyaretnam, Singapore's former solicitor general Mr Francis Seow (now in exile in the US), Singapore's leading corporate lawyer Mr Tang Liang Hong (now in exile in Australia), and Dr Chee Soon Juan, who remains bankrupted and unable to stand for elections.

These are well known democrats who stood up against Lee Kuan Yew, who had openly declared in 2003 that, "If we had considered them serious political figures, we would not have kept them politically alive for so long. We could have bankrupted them earlier." Is this not what the generals in Burma are doing while loudly proclaiming to the world that there will be "free and fair" elections in the country before the end of the year?

While Singapore leaders are shedding crocodile tears and sermonizing the Burmese generals on the need for free and fair elections, is it not appropriate for them to look at their own backyard?

When Singapore's Senior Minister Goh Chok Tong met the Burmese generals, including Than Shwe, last year, he urged them not to allow the ongoing trial of Suu Kyi to affect the national reconciliation process and to make sure that the proposed elections are free and fair.

It is better for Goh to take a hard look at himself in the mirror: he will then be able to see the ugly features that include a well documented law providing for indefinite detention without trial, under which detainees are subject to regular physical and mental torture. It is also common in Singapore to prosecute opposition politicians for speaking in public and distributing flyers; laws that are no different from the Burmese junta.

Goh Chok Tong's "advice" is double speak at best. What right has he got to advise the generals when the same despicable acts are committed at every election in Singapore? Are elections in Singapore free and fair in the first place? Is the media in Singapore free and pluralistic for the voters to be informed before they go to the polls to choose their representatives to parliament?

Burma's media laws are the strictest in the world, and so are Singapore's, the most notorious being the Newspapers and Printing Presses Act that gives sweeping powers, including the appointment of editors to the 14 daily newspapers that are all under the control of the PAP government. Burma is ranked 171 out of 175 countries in the recent Reporters Without Borders Press Freedom Index. Singapore is also in the miserable position of 133, several ranks below that of even Angola and Congo.

The Singapore Press Holdings, whose chairman was a former deputy prime minister, runs all the newspapers of which its flagship daily is the Straits Times. It's a known fact that intelligence operatives masquerade as reporters and journalists in Singapore's media scene. The Straits Times has its equivalent in Burma, the New Light of Myanmar, which is nothing but a mouthpiece of the military regime.

Similarities between the autocratic rule in Singapore and the equally notorious regime in Burma are endless. Learning from Singapore on how to perpetuate one party rule through sham elections is a natural progression for Burma under the bloodthirsty generals.

Burning Man

Gloria Frym

She prepares her daughter and ten other young women for Burning Man (though it is her idea of hell). Water: they'll have to bring all they'll use, at least 1.5 gallons per person per day. How to live in the desert (of late summer). "She'll have a lot of (I've heard) sex there," (did you buy condoms and lubricant?), "I'm told." "She only wanted me to streak her hair green" (so why think about sex?). Baby wipes are helpful for sand in the (wrong) creased places. There be no shoots and leaves, no berries. What do they do in such a climate (under the tents)? They slather themselves with creams and oils (she shudders to give up her only child to the gods of who knows what). The nights get cold, the blankets get warm. So much music, movement, smoke, and porta-potties. Wear big skirts like native women who squat anywhere protected. Take a spade. Yet the women are travelling in an RV (it can't fit all ten). They will stay up all night dancing (and everything else) and sleep all day in the shelter of the vehicle. Which have fans and a bathroom (though where could it hook up to water in the desert, it can't convert sand to liquid) (there are generators) (this generation has them) (they are careful) (the birthrate is declining) they are smart (why else did their parents send them to good schools, wait-listed for better ones). They are even graduate students. Some have prepared for the LSAT, the GAMSAT, the GRE, the CBSE (why aren't they studying instead of going off to burn an effigy) (like some cult wacked religious group Kool-Aid drinkers). They were raised secularly, by hand, tenderly fed bits of croissant before they could speak (English), protected from SIDS, took archery lessons, soccered, ballet, gymnastics, horseback riding, ice skated, yogaed, capoieraed, violined, pianoed, steel drummed, swam, snowboarded, skied, cycled (not bicycled),through their beautiful, unblemished years. (All that equipment in the closets plus helmets.) Strolled through parks, disembarked from Snuglies♪ on the greenest grasses (free of chemical fertilizers) practiced walking with outstretched hands until the fall.

And what about Burning Woman? Not time yet? (Just why burn anything where the rainfall is less than an inch a year?)

When daughter returns, the basement is flooded (father and mother know how to sump pump), a hurricane causes two million to evacuate the Louisiana Coast (clearly not the place for burning a man in effigy unless the festival were retitled Drowning Man which would take care of water boarding, failure to respond) (what was GWB doing during Katrina? So close to nothing we can't remember) (no desire to rebuild the terrible blown apart mold-ridden parts of the city the levees that hold the waters of the mighty Miss at bay) (the deserted fantastic streets once loved into real the gulf) (the local) (the language) (N'Awlins) (the people).

All the Time

Gloria Frym

A life of always busy. Dinner on Tuesday, no can do. Lunch on Sunday, no, teach cycling class. Breakfast on Friday, not a chance. Every appointment made cancelled remade postponed remade, and negotiated until appointments are scratched out question marks on other people's calendars. Perhaps next month. Or after the new year. One suspects that many persons enjoy being deep disembodied voices instead of bodies. The busyness is real but the person may not be. That one over there is in a huge hurry. America was made for him and by him. A New York minute is too slow. He cannot even stop to use an adjective. His modifiers are always adverbs. Reading is too slow, the words don't move. That one has several degrees, so in another lifetime must have read. Now speed lives.

A lovely afternoon in Havana, aboard a ferry that shuttles across the bay to a small town of great interest. The ferry is filled with bicycles in special racks. Their riders stand and look at the view. One cyclist overhears two tourists speaking English; he joins them, he is an English teacher. The three speak during the leisurely voyage, floating away toward a new place. By the time they have disembarked, the cyclist invites the tourists to join him in a visit to old friends. This is the way we Cubans are, he says. They walk slowly up the main street of the town, passing its denizens who sit at tables fanning themselves, eating ice cream, drinking colas, staring, smiling at passersby. They walk and they walk, and the tourists are dripping with sweat from the exceptional heat of the afternoon sun. The buildings of the town are low slung and the road is slightly uphill. When at last they reach their destination, they are greeted by the cyclist's friends and invited into the home of perfect strangers. The entire family appears. The guests are given the best seats in the house, the couch. Everyone is introduced. Some speak English, some do not—one speaks whatever one likes. Coffee is made and offered. One of the tourists offers to go out and buy cokes and beer. When he returns, the conversation enlivens, poetry is recited, and the Cubans are thrilled to exchange ideas. They have all the time in the world. They put on a tape of rumba music, the cyclist asks the woman tourist to dance, she demurs and says she doesn't know how to rumba, he says he'll teach her. They move in one spot of the small living room next to a pink 1950s television as the others drink and watch. A slow tune comes on. The other tourist becomes slightly jealous watching her held so tightly by the cyclist. Hours pass in stories and laughter and questions and answers. The family wants to take the tourists to the pride and joy of their town, which is El Museo y El Monumento de Lenin. They all walk to a one-room museum on a hill, which contains a variety of Lenin's artifacts. Then they walk down a step set of steps to a large George Segal-like set of statues of workers surrounding a gigantic statue of Lenin. The tourists take photographs of the group standing in front of the monument—it's a historical moment. The family invites the tourists for dinner. They keep a couple of chickens in the backyard. They would kill a precious commodity to accommodate their new friends. Dusk is nearing, the tourists feel they should not impose, and make an excuse about needing to get back to Havana to meet friends. Perhaps six or seven hours have passed. The new friends take twenty minutes to hug and say goodbye. They promise to write. The tourists would like to give the family some supplies they have brought as presents, and arrange for the cyclist to meet them the next day at their hotel. The tourists leave on the ferry back to Havana. They have a leisurely daiquiri that costs half a month's salary for a Cuban. They have another. They go back to their hotel. And they sleep a long, slow sleep, very slowly.

Early in the morning, the telephone rings. The operator says a cyclist is calling for them at the front door of the lobby. He has taken the ferry, the man tourist says to the woman, already, and of course, they won't let Cubans into the hotel. The woman says you go down; it would take me a long time to get organized. Please give the cyclist everything in that bag. The man quickly dresses and goes down to meet the cyclist and finds the entire family, in their best attire, waiting outside the door of the hotel, waiting patiently, for their new friends.

Time Trip Back to the 1960s
(an excerpt from *Alien Journal*)

Lee Balan

The inside of the Gashouse was dark and musty. A bathtub with claw-feet was in the middle of the floor. A naked man sat in the tub and read a poem. Some sort of stage was behind the tub, closed off by a wall of curtains. There were a few old couches and lots of tables of various sizes with wooden chairs occupied by beatniks who were absorbed in the mellow sounds of jazz that floated through the room. The black walls were covered with protest art. Several anti-war sculptures stood around the room like pieces of collateral damage.

Hippies arrived later—dressed in tie-dyed clothes, listening to Bob Dylan and Mick Jagger—exchanging flowers and food. Everyone began to dance. The place became a kaleidoscope of colorful reflections.

The sound of a pipe organ intruded with *Amazing Grace* and dusty curtains were pulled up to the ceiling like seagulls yanked into the air. Crenulated drapes were revealed, and more curtains—opening, opening—unveiling a spectacle: a gold foil Stairway to Heaven rose on pink, crepe clouds. A painting of Judy Canova (star of 1940s comedies) wistfully hung from a star in a painted sky. The giant staircase slowly turned like a spiral corkscrew drilling a hole through the starry ceiling. David was completely absorbed by the funky spectacle.

A purple lizard dressed as a Ring Master stood in front of the staircase and eulogized, "Welcome everyone. Welcome to the parade of history."

People in fantastic costumes posed on the revolving staircase. One man was dressed like the Roman Coliseum complete with Christians being fed to the lions. Someone was dressed like the Great Pyramid of Cheops. Every costume was an outrageous miracle or an obscene drama. The Hanging Gardens of Babylon swung back and forth to *Steam Heat* sung by Peggy Lee. The Tower of Babel crumbled like a skyscraper in an earthquake.

Groucho Marx chased Lady Astor through the mayhem. The giant heads of Easter Island nodded and smiled. Menhirs and dolmens sang *That Old Black Magic* in the middle of Stonehenge. David's mind was playing tricks—he was confused by lavish elaborations.

"Confusion often leads to illumination," quoth the ravine—the ravenous ravine that devoured the immortal liver of Prometheus. Confusion gave way to the Three Stooges performing Bertolt Brecht—gave way to Judy Canova who split atoms with her horse laugh. She rose above the confusion like a crescendo. Everything else was just confetti.

The room grew dim and quiet. Lights flickered below the level of perception transforming the walls and floor into glowing lace. Space shifted into a cave of living fiber. David lay cradled on the gently vibrating floor.

He was drawn to a few people sitting on a hill overlooking a central garden. As the spaces in the room converged he found himself next to the group. He was offered wine that exploded on his tongue causing bubbles to collide in his brain. Invisible fingers plucked his ribs like a harp. David's backbone slipped and shimmied like a nervous snake. A clown cavorted in the garden and he couldn't stop laughing.

Mitchell Waldman

a winter morning's mantra

feel the hum
feel the strum
feel the wheat
harmony
of the New Day
spring sky
on a winter morning
one foot after the other
after the other
soothing sounds
of waves splashing
against the beach

homeless men and women
walking into homes of smiling faces

for shelter
for food
banks canceling 32 dollar late fees
doors being held open
"After you."
No, after you."
traffic accidents dotted with
"Sorries" and apologetic smiles
soldiers laying down rifles
pointed at strangers
at fathers and sons
angry eyes calmed
in the sea
of spring's
surprise
appearance

but
don't be deceived
dense gray clouds
angry stares
crouching
hiding
in the distance
icy breezes
locked inside our heads

people been waiting
for the New Day
for centuries
waiting
banging heads walls
praying

and it always turns out the same—
new boss same as the old boss
spite before right
might before night

but don't give up hope
feel the hum
the strum
feel the wheat
the spring's rising sun
feel the Day
the New Day
and let us pray—
maybe this time
oh, maybe this time.

Mitchell Waldman

Alien Life

Who dropped me on this planet?—
I want to know.
Who left me here without the instruction manual,
without the translation dictionary?
Come get me, Mom?
Why did you leave me here all alone?
Who needs Kryptonite
when you have human emotions to deal with
a factor so long forgotten on this planet—
sex, death, life, nothing more here than a
series of ads for Nike, Coke, Levis, Safe Sex

not like back home, on our planet where
feelings were understood
the spirit was acknowledged as supreme
and there was no Video Shack
no Hustler Babe of the Month
no 900 numbers
no "Will Work For Food" signs
no unemployment checks
no dribble down your shirt front economics
no nuclear missiles
dead lakes
mansions on the hill
caviar and truffles
no, none of that.
Why was I left here

as some observer of a great experiment gone bad?
I've seen enough, Ma,
Scotty, beam me up,
Please!!

Mitchell Waldman

Nineteen

He was nineteen
dying in a field
in a foreign land.
That was all he knew.
He wasn't feeling brave
but only afraid
as he felt the life
slipping out of him.

He didn't know who was right
or who was wrong
as they argued about it
in the grocery stores
in the newspapers

at the filling stations
and he lay dying
in this field of green.

He didn't feel as if it were an honor to die
he didn't feel dignified
or proud,
just scared,
a boy longing for home.

He didn't know anything now
just the pain;
he wasn't thinking about bleeding heart liberals
or staunch conservatives
only about all the things he wouldn't see
he wouldn't do in his life
now that it would all be over so soon
and the fear of the unknown

of what was soon to come.

He didn't know much about politics about "stand firm"
or "the right plan"
he didn't know
which candidate
was better for the country
(now he would never get the chance to vote).

He only knew
he was nineteen
and he was going to die
before he had a chance
to live
and he wasn't really sure
why.

Fortunate Son

Mitchell Waldman

Delores Leary picked up the baseball mitt setting on the undisturbed blue cover of the single bed. It was one of two beds in the room, the one that her son, Andy, had occupied when he'd been there. She stroked the worn brown leather palm of the mitt and brought it close to her face to smell its musky scent. Then she closed her eyes and found herself traveling back, back to those innocent days, driving Andy and Ricky to their little league games, sitting in the bleachers, watching the two of them run across the sun-bleached field in their green Dorsey Dodge uniforms. She'd been so proud, watching her little guys, cheering them on every time one of them came to bat or a ball was hit in their direction. And she'd always been there to encourage them with a smile or a pat on the back when one of them dropped a ball, struck out, or was thrown out trying to steal a base.

She buried her face in the leather, fell across the bed, and wept silent tears. She remembered his face, those eyes, that smile, that beacon of unadulterated light that seemed like it would burn forever. But that was then.

A car commercial was playing on the television. Delores lit a cigarette and winced. When *it* had happened she'd taken up smoking again after having quit for ten years. The tune in the background was Creedence Clearwater Revival's *Fortunate Son*. Ironic, she thought. A large flag, ghostly, superimposed in the background, was waving in the wind as a midnight blue sports car drove by fast, dust flying up by the roadside. The advertisers missed the point. It was an antiwar song but they'd distorted it for their own use, to sell cars, all American cars, made to a great extent in Japan.

She thought of Andy, her own very *mis*fortunate son.

Another ad came on, this one for the Marines. A line of strong, iron jawed men in dress blues marched and saluted while the crowd clapped and cheered in the background waving flags. Patriotism—what was that? The heading ran across the screen: *A few good men. Are you man enough to fit the bill?*

Man enough. She couldn't take it. She felt dizzy, grasped for the remote and hit the red button. And then there was only silence in the house. A strange, reverberating stillness. And the swishing of cars outside in the rain.

What had he been thinking when he'd decided to join up? Had he been caught up by the flag waving, the propaganda? A few good men, a few good men for what? To die? It was bullshit, pure bullshit. It wasn't the advertisers—sons going over there, still children, scared children, not knowing what the hell they were doing, acting like men, prey to their macho preachings. Boys wanted to be men. Of course. So this was how they could prove themselves. Is that what Andy had thought? That this would make him a man?

He was sitting next to Ricky at the dinner table playing with his peas, moving them to the back of his plate. He hadn't touched his lamb chops. It wasn't like Andy not to eat. He was just sitting there, staring at his plate. Meanwhile blond-haired Ricky, a year younger than his brother, was shoveling the last bite of his chop into his mouth, chewing greedily, smacking his belly and belching, this big goofy smile on his face.

"God, Rick, that's gross!" Delores said. "Where did you learn your manners from, the zoo?"

Ricky laughed, but Andy wasn't reacting at all, still staring obliviously at his plate. The younger boy stopped laughing and stared at his brother.

"Okay, Andy boy, what is it?" Delores asked. What's wrong with my little boy?"

Andy looked up at his mother, his eyebrows pulled together, his eyes narrowed to two small slits. "Maybe that's it, Mom. I'm not your little boy anymore. I'm eighteen. Or haven't you noticed?"

"Yeah, yeah, you're eighteen. Let me tell you something. You'll always be my little boy, even when you're eighty and I'm dead."

"Oh, very nice, Mom," Ricky said, and started laughing.

Andy was still staring at her with his deadpan look. Then he spilled it: "Joe Martin's joining the Army." Joe Martin was his best friend. They'd been Cub Scouts together, gone fishing together, then, when they were older, had gone on double dates together.

"He is? What does his mother say about it?"

"Jesus, Mom, that's the whole point. What can she say about it? Joe's a man now."

"Just because you're eighteen and you've had a smoke and a beer and maybe got laid doesn't necessarily qualify you for membership in the Man Club. Does his mother still cook his meals, do his laundry for him, pick up after him?"

"You're missing the point, Mom. Joe's joining up, and...I think I just might, too. What with all this terrorist shit happening and 9/11 and all the Arabs..." There was a moment of shock—her heart was racing and she couldn't breathe, couldn't move or say a word. She thought of how he had looked dressed in his blue Cub Scout uniform with the gold neck kerchief. There was a picture in their foyer of Andy and Joe in these uniforms, arms around each other grinning. Joe freckled and missing one of his front teeth, Andy, hat on crooked, covering a brown mop of hair, crossing his eyes, acting generally goofy and bright like the star that he had seemed to Delores in those days, the brightest star in her sometimes ink black sky. It seemed like only yesterday. How could she be listening to the same boy now, grown up, or almost grown up, talking about "plans," things that no mother could listen to without her heart palpitating, words that no mother could bear to hear?

"I've got to do my share," he said, jaw set. "For all of us." He sounded like some stranger who had walked in the front door and sat himself down at her kitchen table.

"Dad served. I want to do my part, too."

Dad, who in Andy's more bitter moments he referred to as "the Sperm Donor." What could she say while the voice inside her head was screaming "No!!!" She took a deep breath and spoke, trying to battle with him, reason with him. "What about college? You were talking about that, about getting an athletic scholarship, going to college, maybe becoming a doctor. And what about how you've always wanted to help people? How are you going to help people by shooting at them?"

"God, Mom, you don't understand! This is doing something for people. For our people. We're talking about our survival here!"

Delores couldn't believe what she was hearing. She shook her head, and put her hand on his cheek. "You really believe that?" Andy pulled away from her.

"Yes, I really believe that." He looked right at her, firmly, not batting a lash. Then he softened some, turned his gaze down, and stared at his hands, his long slender fingers stretched out on the table top. Suddenly he didn't look so grown up, he didn't look quite so sure of himself. "And, as for school, that can wait. Anyway, I don't know, my grades generally suck and I have no idea what I really want to do. Plus there's the New GI Bill. Sergeant Conners said that would help out financially when I get out.'

When I get out. It echoed in her ears.

If you get out, a voice in her head corrected. This thought came out sooner than she could process it, making her whole body shudder. This was her baby she was thinking about. She felt sick to her stomach, like she was going to vomit, rose from the table and bolted for the bathroom.

"Mom, you all right in there? You didn't die or anything, did ya'?'

She got off her knees, flushed the toilet, smoothed down her blouse and looked at herself in the mirror, trying a smile on for her boys. Not a very convincing one, she was sure, but it would have to do.

"I'm fine, Andy, just must've been something I ate." Then she opened the door and tried that smile out on them, Andy standing there with the concerned look, hands on his hips, and his "little brother," the body builder who was at least twice as wide as Andy, bending over, putting his hand gently on his mother's back, saying, "Are you all right, Mom? Are you sure you're all right?"

The phone call came on a Tuesday evening. She was watching a game show, Hollywood Squares. She watched anything other than the news these days. Comedies especially, love stories. Even cartoons and game shows. Anything to keep from hearing the real stuff, the news about the war.

It was a Sergeant Young who called. He didn't say why but he wanted to come see her. Personally. She was terrified when she heard him say that. It could only mean one thing, couldn't it? Or maybe she was just jumping to conclusions. Maybe she'd seen one war movie too many.

When the knock came at the door she didn't know what to do. She continued to sort the mail and papers lying on the table in her kitchen, afraid to move. Again the knock. The vibrations of the BOOM BOOM BOOM reverberated through her body like an electrical shock. She stacked her papers and envelopes neatly, brushed back her hair, and walked slowly, feeling her insides quiver as she approached the door. She felt like she was watching someone else as she turned the bolt lock, pulled open the door and stared at a soldier in dress blues standing there with a somber look, hands clasped in front of his belt. She sighed, while the woman she was watching asked the man to come in.

He was sitting on the couch, a good-looking 20ish man with a brush of blond hair on the top of his head. What was he doing here? Why wasn't he sitting somewhere in some office, staring safely at some computer screen, or working at a toy store customer service desk, shining those blue eyes on unhappy customers, apologizing for the air gun that didn't fire right, rather than sitting here now doing what he was about to do?

Andy was eight years old preparing for his role in a class room production of *Sleeping Beauty*. He was playing the part of the Handsome Prince mainly because no other boy in the class had had the courage to do so. Delores tried to imagine him sticking his hand straight up in the air while the other boys tittered behind their hands or stared down at their desks, trying to avoid the gaze of their teacher, Mrs. Bowman, after she'd called for volunteers to fill the role. How proud she'd been of him when he'd told her about it. Not that he hadn't been afraid to. He had never been one to shy away from his fears. He'd learned his lines the week before the play and when time came to deliver, he'd strode right up onto the stage and delivered the lines expertly, without flinching.

And when the time had come for him to "do his part," as he'd said, he hadn't flinched either. She wished he would have flinched a little sometimes. But, with Andy, it had always been charge right into it, without question. He never lacked decisiveness, that was for sure. And look where it had gotten him. Just look.

The young man sat on the sofa across from Delores. She had her manners on, asked him if he wanted something to drink. He smiled and said a glass of water would be fine. It was a hot day. One of those 95 in the shade types of days.

She walked very carefully into the kitchen, maintaining control, opened the refrigerator door, poured the water from the jug, closed the refrigerator door, and walked just as carefully back to the living room. Her hand shook only slightly as she brought the glass to the young man.

She'd forgotten his name, although she was sure he had told her when he'd appeared at the door. Suddenly, it seemed so important to know his name, like her son's very life hinged on knowing it.

"I'm sorry," she said, leaning over, handing the trembling glass to the man, "your name was ..."

"Just call me Derron, Mrs. Leary."

"Derron," she said, feeling nothing at all. Just numbness. Like this was some sort of strange dream, not quite real.

He took the glass from her, took a long drink from it, wiped his brow, and set the glass on the end table next to the couch. Then he folded his hands together and looked across at Delores. "The reason I'm here, Mrs. Leary, is that your son, Andy, is what we call Missing in Action.' He paused for a moment watching. She sat in her chair, hands neatly folded on her lap, staring at the young man, watching his mouth move. Feeling nothing still, numb from head to toe. Staring at this man, this boy, because that's all he was, a boy who'd been given the task of telling the unspeakable to the mother of another boy he probably never even met. While older men, politicians and rogues who planned all the wars, the attacks, sat in comfy leather chairs, she imagined, smoking cigars, and drinking twenty year old brandy, thinking up their next stratagem, not thinking of the lives of these boys and their families that would be affected by what to them were games, mere games. In her mind she saw them laughing and carrying on, maybe tossing in a dirty joke or an ethnic joke here or there. Maybe one about Arabs, no doubt one about Arabs, Iraqis. There always had to be someone to kick around, to blame for things, to look down on. Someone to feel better than. To stomp on. But we're all people, she thought, aren't we? If we kill one of theirs, if we kill fifty of theirs, there are still possibly fifty sets of parents on their side who have lost a son. Just like her—Missing in Action. She knew what that meant, even though he went on to explain: "This means nothing more than that his whereabouts are currently unaccounted for."

She nodded stiffly, only because it was what he wanted her to do. But, then, she put her head down and she couldn't help herself. She started to weep. Sitting straight upright, her hands positioned along the blue denim covering her upper thighs, and crying like a fountain, silently. Weeping tears that she'd held for hours since she'd gotten the call and knew what was coming.

Andy was dead. She knew he was and nothing that this or any other person could say would change that. "Missing in Action" just meant they hadn't found him yet. She showed the Sergeant to the door. He turned sharply when she opened the screen door and shook her hand. "We'll let you know when we have more information. And don't be overly concerned. He may just be misplaced for the moment."

Misplaced. What a strange way to put it and what a terrible, cowardly thing to do, to lie to a dead boy's mother. She felt like saying something, the anger building in her, but said only, "Thank you, Sergeant," and watched him walk stiffly, cap in hand, to his car.

Just misplaced. She almost wanted to laugh aloud, cackle rudely at the boy, but the hollow pit in her chest prevented her from doing so. It was the place where her heart had been. Her misplaced heart.

She had started working at the high school when Andy had just entered his freshman year. Why had she taken the job there after losing the job at the real estate agency? Because she couldn't stand to be too far away from him, to lose a grip on her little boy?

In four short years that probably felt like decades to Andy, she'd watched him mature into a young man in the halls of that high school. She'd seen him gain confidence and muscle and add a swagger to his step as he approached the girls his age, who all seemed to adore him. He'd been the quarterback on the football team, a pitcher in baseball. Some college was bound to pick him up, award him a sports scholarship, despite his grades, which hadn't been too bad, really. He was good. So why had he shut the door on them, shut the door on his education and gone the way he'd gone?

Some mistakes you can change, some things you can go back and fix but this, as it seemed to turn out, was not one of them. *But one life to give to my country*. Nathan Hale. The fabled phrase being that he'd regretted that he'd but one life to give to his country. Only twenty one when he was hanged by the British. She wasn't sure why she remembered these facts all of the sudden, this remnant of her own studies long since past, but the words rang with a shrill clarity through her brain as she sipped her morning coffee and read the headlines about the war, about Iraq, a place no one in their right mind would go to of their own volition. A hostile land, but a land filled with people, people like she and Andy, with mothers and sons and brothers and fathers. Who breathed the same air, needed food and water, love and understanding. Killing each other for what? Some political agenda? Differences of opinion? For private capitalistic interests of certain politicos afraid that they and their buddies might lose a share of their profits? For the flexing of the almighty male muscle? Aggression, ape-like shows of brutality? King of the hill politics? Terrorizing a country because of a few bad apples who just so happened, unfortunately, to have been in power at the time and had been, ironically, terrorizing their own citizens? Not clear. Made no sense. Police force of the world USA. Andy wasn't a Fortunate Son. And Delores sure as hell didn't feel like a Fortunate Mother these days either. No way, not at all. All she saw of the world now was through tear stained eyes. it was like gazing through a glass of water, a river of tears.

She didn't know why she called him—Jerry, her ex, the role model for her boy to sacrifice himself for a war he knew nothing about. He, like his father, had gone to fight other men's battles, fighting for secret political and businessmen's agendas behind the red white and blue shining in the sun as a facade for the real reasons for these battles of power. Why did men always start wars? To overcome insecurities about the sizes of their penises? To show that their muscles were bigger than those of the other testosterone laced warriors?

When Jerry pulled up to the door in his beat up Chevy Blazer, she was almost sorry she'd called him. What had she been thinking? Their marriage had been a sham for a long time. Ever since the war, since he'd come home with the severed arm. He'd lost more than an arm then. He'd lost his humanity, his spirit. He was not the man he had been, but seemed, after Vietnam, to be just a shell of that person. Still she had stayed with him for a long time, too long. Long enough to give birth to Andy and Ricky. She'd felt guilty about it, somehow, that he had gotten injured. She took care of him. But why? After twelve years of marriage she asked herself that question and realized how ridiculous her guilt was. She had not committed war, she had not ripped off his arm in the middle of a fire fight. She had done nothing but absorb his pain for twelve long, sad, empty years. And, after twelve years she had packed Jerry's bags one sunny autumn day and told him to move out. He must have seen it coming—he knew they didn't have a functioning marriage anymore—because all he did was nod and pick up the bags, a hang dog look on his face, and walked out the door.

And this was the man that Andy had been inspired by. He hadn't known his father before the shell shock of war, how he had smiled and laughed and imitated his high school teachers. He had, in fact, been the class clown. And after the war, if he cracked a smile once in a month it was something of an aberration, a miracle almost, the ghost of the Jerry she had known in the past.

She stood by the front door, peering out the little window, watching him, in his Cubs cap, slam the door of his Blazer, walk around the car slowly, and trudge up the walk. When he got to the steps, she opened the door before he could ring the bell. He almost fell into the house, but caught himself, his good arm swinging in the air—he looked like a high wire walker, catching his balance and straightening his body in one fluid motion. Jerry could be more graceful looking than she'd ever suspected, but after years of doing the one armed man routine, she figured he'd mastered it pretty well.

"Got a beer?" were the first words out of his mouth. Not "Hello," or "How're the boys?" or "How are you?," nothing as cordial as that. Just, "Got a beer?," like he stopped over there every other day.

"Uh, no, Jerry. Sorry about that. No beer." He pulled his cap off and stared at her, looking confused for a moment, then shrugged. "Okay," he said. His reddish hair was thinning and mussed, he had what looked like two days of stubble on his face, and was wearing one of those red checked flannel shirts that he seemed so fond of. It could have been the same one she saw him in the last time he'd been there (what had it been two, three months ago when he'd actually shown up to visit with Ricky, take him to a baseball game?).

He walked into the living room and dropped down on the couch, like he belonged there, like he still lived there. Delores just stared at the man, wondering who he was, who he had become, and wondering why on earth she had called him here, why she had thought, in a moment of insanity, that he could somehow calm her fears, soothe her sorrows, her feelings of loss.

"If you wanted some beer, you should have brought your own," Delores said, hands on hips. "Anyway, this isn't a fucking social call. It's about our son. It's about Andy. He's missing."

She was staring at him, looking for some reaction in his face, in those foggy eyes. "Missing?" was all he said, like he hadn't served in Nam, like he had no understanding of what the word meant.

"Yes, Jerry, missing, like Missing in Action, MIA, gone, gone, gone." She raised her hand to her face to cover the tears and to block out everything—she didn't want to see the world, and certainly didn't want to see Jerry's reaction, him feeling sorry for her, he of all people. In a moment though, through the silence of the room, the heaviness of her sobs in a room decorated with cheery daisy covered wallpaper (what had she been thinking when she did that?), she felt his thick hand on her back tentatively, and he said in his breathy voice, "It's okay, Delores. It'll be all right." To which she reacted violently, shaking his hand off of her, staring at his dumb, emotionless face, and shouting, ""No, Jerry, it will not be all right, it was never all right! You are not all right—look what they did to you—your son is not all right, this world is not all right as long as we're sending our boys to slaughter for no logical reason!"

He was staring back at her now, arms by his sides, his amputated limp hanging there in the tied off shirt, a hopeless, useless appendage, a reminder of what Jerry seemed to have become—a hollow, hopeless, defenseless man. He looked like he was about to cry, and Delores was immediately sorry, but she wouldn't, she couldn't say it, just held her breath waiting for him to go, just go. After a few minutes he got the idea, picked up his baseball cap off the couch, and mumbled, "I'm sorry, I was just trying to help." He stood there, looking at her and stumbled toward the door without another word. Delores watched him and calmly said, as he was opening the screen door, "He's dead, Jerry. Our son is dead." He didn't seem to hear it or chose not to as the screen door slammed behind him and he walked stiffly, like some sort of slow monster, long since robbed of his powers, back to his car.

Days went by, then weeks without any further word from the Army, from Sergeant Young. The war went on, more reports of the constantly increasing death toll of American soldiers, and of prisoners being beheaded, coming every day. It got to the point where she didn't want to hear any more. She just wanted to stuff her fingers in her ears, and shut her eyes tight, not hear or see another word about war. Everywhere she went—the grocery store, the hairdresser, the gas station—people were talking about it. How many more of their kids would die? The argument over whether the President had been right in invading the country and whether it was unpatriotic to question his intent in getting the terrorists. She wanted to move to a different country, a place where her son would not have been sent to such a place to lay his life on the line. But it was too late for that now anyway. Too late, too late, too late.

So what do you do when you think your son is dead? What can you do is the question? You go on through the motions, throwing loads of laundry into the washing machine, clearing dishes from the dishwasher, sweeping the floor, cutting the grass, making coffee, reading the newspaper, like everything's okay, everything's normal. But nothing's okay, nothing's normal, nothing's the same. The world has been spun on its side, and it's like you're a top spinning, looking for something to grab onto to regain your balance, but there's nothing to grab, nothing at all. You close your eyes and listen to the cars swish by, hearing the rain water splashing in the street. And, as the sun falls and the shadowy lines of night creep into the solitude of your room, you wonder if the next person who knocks on the door or the next voice on the phone will be that of your son, your missing son.

She heard nothing, but was afraid to call the Sergeant, afraid almost to breathe. She played a game, acted as if Andy were on a vacation somewhere. She even imagined where he was, at a beach somewhere, Florida maybe. She would close her eyes and imagined watching him lay a towel on the hot sand, see the perspiration sliding down his cheek and chin. Imagining him with his buddies, sneaking beers out of a small cooler and making cracks about some of the girls walking by in their skimpy bikinis. "Get a load of that one," she could hear him say, tipping his head towards a blonde haired girl in a hot pink bikini, hitting his friend, Joe, with the back of his hand. "I'd love to get a load of that, are you kiddin'?" And then they were laughing, crazy carefree laughter, the way they had used to, the way he had, before...before....

It was just after their last football game of the season. Their senior year. Their last football game. It was about one o'clock in the morning when she'd heard a ruckus outside, swept the lace curtains in her bedroom back and peered out the window to see Andy and Ricky and Joe walking arm in arm, laughing and singing the lyrics to "Satisfaction" at the top of their lungs, slipping and swaying down the sidewalk, this huge six legged drunken teenage monster boy. It was a wonder people weren't yelling out the window and that a police car wasn't rolling up beside them to give them a talking to. It was all she could do to get her robe wrapped around her and hop down the stairs when she heard the front door open and the three boys tumble into her foyer laughing and singing and falling onto the floor. Punching each other and howling and being boys. Andy among the pile on the floor with his broad grin and deep laugh, long arms and legs sprawled by his side like a helpless infant. Not a fragment of anything but innocence in his big brown eyes. She'd meant to yell at them, scold them for drinking, tell them they were being way too loud and disrespectful, that people were sleeping. But seeing them, seeing Andy like that, she'd just melted, stood there in the doorway watching them with her arms crossed in front of her, a stern look painted on her face. It was all she could do to stop from laughing. Taking it all in, their youth, their innocence, their exuberance. Drinking it in with her eyes, this wide smile on her face, feeling like her face was going to crack she was smiling so widely then.

And that moment was so brief, just a minute sliver of the pie, a sparkling fleck of dust in the nighttime, a single moment in the infinite moments of time.

She would trudge to work every day at the high school, where she worked in the office. She no longer felt like the young woman she had once been, who rushed headlong into the new day, excited to meet the challenges awaiting her. Now it was like life had become a series of motions repeated on a daily basis. There no longer seemed to be any point in any of it. And her mind was always on Andy. There was a hole inside of her. It wasn't just her son, but it felt like her heart was also missing in action.

She was driving to work on a lightly traveled road and saw a fuzzy gray object streak in front of her car. She swerved to miss it, almost running off the road, and squealed her brakes. She got out of the car, shaking, looking back at the space where she had been. The sun was shining and the birds were chirping from the overhanging trees, which swayed in the gentle summer breeze. In the middle of the road lay a small squirrel motionless on his side, his eyes closed, his tiny little paws curled up under his little jaw. And then there was the shock—his snow white belly. It was totally unexpected. She had assumed squirrels were all just gray or brown or something in between. She had never really given them much thought. She walked toward the animal cautiously, shaking at the thought that she had killed this innocent creature. Tears running down her cheeks, then sobbing.

There was the sound of a car approaching. The little animal was lying right on the double yellow line. She couldn't let the remnant of her violent act be made even worse. So she stood like a guard in front of the little animal, her feet planted firmly, her arms raised, palms forward as a small red sports car approached and squealed its brakes to a stop, just a foot from where she was standing, where she would not budge. Two young men in business suits yelled at her, one yelling "Get out of the road, crazy lunatic!!", the other yelling "Loony bitch!" Okay, she was a lunatic, a loony bitch and she was sure she must look like a sight, a fright, her mascara all running down her cheeks now from the tears, but she didn't care. She had murdered the little squirrel with her monster machine and the least she could do was give it a decent burial. The tremors ran through her body as the tiny red car sputtered off. She pulled off her sweater and carefully bent down to the spot where he lay, so peacefully, so sadly, the birds singing his eulogy, the sun warming the remains of his soul. Did animals have souls? She didn't know, but she assumed they did. She got right next to the gray squirrel. She was not afraid, bent down and stroked its soft white belly, so naked looking in the daylight, in the bright sun, the tears streaming down her cheeks now. She stared at him for thirty seconds or so, then wrapped him up like an infant in her sweater and held the tiny animal close to her breast.

Once inside the car, she put the sweater on the passenger seat beside her and pulled her cell phone out of her purse. She dialed the school's number and told the vice principal, Anne McCoffrey, that she had had a little accident. No, she was all right, she said. Just a little shook up. She would be in a little later. Then she turned the car around and, her hands still shaking on the wheel, headed back home. There she would get out her shovel and, the tears still flowing, would try not to think about what she was really thinking, dig a three foot deep hole in her garden behind the tomato plants and plant her little friend, the innocent victim, the one who hadn't known, who hadn't seen her coming. Lying him in a place of peace and, she hoped, eternal rest.

Two months after Sergeant Young came to her door and shattered her world, she could not think straight, could not go an hour without crying or feeling like she was about to cry. She called the Army every day, sometimes twice, three times a day and the answer was always the same: No news.

She was falling apart.

Sometimes it didn't seem like she could make it through another day.

At night she would awaken three, sometimes four times. Sometimes it seemed like it was for no reason at all. But there was a reason—a waiting, an expectancy of something. Something like Andy rushing through the door, that big wide grin on his face as he would through his muscled arms around her and she would say, softly, almost to herself, patting his back lightly: "You made it, you finally made it home."

Other times there were nightmares. Grotesque images of someone who looked like Andy, starting as a teenager, with the gleaming smile, the bright clear eyes, the reddened cheeks from spending a crisp winter day playing out in the snow and ice. And after that the face would change before her eyes, melt almost so that it was dripping, misshapen, like a melted candle and the smile would turn downward, disappear altogether into the bottom of his chin. And his body would become deformed, parts of limbs hanging, looking more like a tattered scarecrow. It was sort of a theme, a recurring dream. The most terrifying of all was when, instead of flying through the door to greet her, wrap his arms around her, he came through the door and reached out for her but had nothing to reach with, lacking arms, only the sockets where they should have been remaining, and as he reached over to hug her, he fell face first to the floor, his face cracking like glass, while she helplessly bent down, weeping, shaking, crying "Andy, are you okay, are you okay, Honey?" And in the midst of all this Ricky would show up with a broom and a dust pan, seemingly without emotion, and sweep the cracked shards of his brother's face into the pan and toss them into the trash, only his brother's torso remaining, lifeless on the floor, a hunk of useless flesh which she clung to, her heart nearing the breaking point, wailing to the ceiling, but there was no one there, no one was listening. What of God, where was he, if he was, and why wouldn't he do something to bring her child back to her?

She would wake up, her body drenched in sweat, her heart pounding and her mind racing, it taking her a minute to realize that no, this had not actually happened, it was just a dream. She would sit up in bed, her arms wrapped around herself, holding herself like a baby. Then, unable to sleep, she would fix herself a cup of tea, turn on the tube, drape a blanket over herself, her cold sweat bringing a chill to her body. If she was having a lucky night she might doze off an hour or two before it was time to wake up again and go through the morning drudgery of getting ready for work. Other nights she wasn't so lucky and would never fall asleep at all, but would prepare herself to work, and drag herself through the day like some sort of awakened corpse, one of the faceless nameless creatures in Dawn of the Dead, walking around that shopping mall aimlessly reaching reaching reaching for something, for nothing, for everything.

She told herself that she was strong, but no one could be this strong. She would talk to friends. Her oldest, dearest friend, Becky, would sit there and hold her and cry with her. They had grown up together, gotten married and had children together and had been close always, sharing their secrets, loves, and hates, their fear and their pain. The pain and fear that comes from raising a child in this world. And when you lose a child—what greater pain does a mother have than that? They were like sisters, holding each other, Becky comforting Delores through the night. But when Becky left the pain was still there, there was no getting rid of it. And Jerry, Jerry was Andy's father, but he was more like a child than anything. He just didn't seem to comprehend. Ricky, you couldn't even talk to him about it.

When she had first told Ricky that Andy was "missing in action," he had just smiled and wrapped his arms around his mother, saying, "Don't worry, Mom. He'll be back. He's just missing. Don't go worrying for nothing." Then, with a smile reminiscent of Andy's, but not quite as broad or convincing, he had walked off to school, whistling, actually whistling, as he'd picked up his books and pushed out the screen door.

And after that there had been little scenes. He was in a total state of denial it seemed. One time sitting next to each other at dinner. The silence heavy between them. Delores watched as Ricky ate, looking at the empty seat beside him. She'd started crying then and Ricky had looked up at her for an instance, seeming almost annoyed at his mother, but then returned his attention to his steak,, his knife and fork poised for attack.

She had said then, "He's not coming home, Ricky. Your brother's dead." In response to which Andy threw his utensils across the room, hitting the wall, stood up and yelled at her, "I'm not going to take this, you acting like this. My brother is not dead. He's missing, missing, that's what the man said, right? Do you know what missing means? They don't know where he is right now, that's all. They didn't say he was dead!" He stormed out of the room then, and out of the house. She would have liked to console him, put her arms around him, and let him sink against her, like he used to, but he was becoming a man in his own right now, seventeen years old. He was no mama's boy anymore. He was at the age where showing your feelings was not allowed, was subject to the ridicule of all your peers.

But that wasn't what bothered Delores Leary. What bothered her most was the thought that maybe he wasn't feeling anything but anger. That maybe he really believed that Andy was still alive. Maybe Ricky was just in a state of total denial. And what would happen when he came out of it? Would he fall, break down? Would he, could he ever be the same without his big brother?

She tossed and turned at night, woke up staring at the clock, dragged herself to work, trying to find any information, any information about Andy, only to find nothing, an emptiness growing inside of her, like a black hole, threatening to swallow her up from the inside out. That was how it felt.

She woke up one morning and she couldn't go on. Couldn't even get out of her bed. She reached for the phone on her night stand and called in sick, gave her excuses and her regrets. Then lay there without an ounce of energy to move, without an ounce of motivation to do so.

Her son stopped in for a moment at her doorway and stared at her, just stared. "You're not going to work today?" he asked, to which she replied. "No, what's the point?"

"Is there anything I can get you?"

"No, nothing." To which he shrugged, shuffled with his hands in his khaki pockets, stared at his feet and mumbled, "Well, guess I gotta go."

"Okay, Sweetie," she said, and then, as he was walking away, without knowing why, said, "Be careful out there." Because that was how she felt. That it was a dangerous world. You couldn't take anything for granted anymore, not a thing.

She spent the day watching television and eating Oreos, dropping napkins and wrappers on her nightstand. A tiny mountain of paper would be there by the end of the day. The television voices, the inane smiles of its subjects, numbed her. It was a make believe world, a world of fantasy. The phone rang several times but she wouldn't answer it.

When Ricky came home from school and stopped in on her he came in slowly, cautiously. "Mom," he said, "are you all right?"

She sighed, as he stood at the side of her bed. "No, Honey, I'm not all right, I'm not I'm not I'm not." She broke down then, crying, and he bent down awkwardly and put one arm around her as she wept in his arms. After a few minutes she took a deep long breath and said, "I'm sorry, Ricky for not being strong for you, for disappointing you." To which Ricky said, "No, Mom, it's all right, you know it's all right. You've been taking care of me, of us, for so long, sometimes we forget that you need taking care of, too." She smiled at him and put her hand on his face. Palm to cheek. "I love you, Ricky, I love you so much," she said, wrapping her arms tightly around her son, closing her eyes as the tears dripped off her cheeks.

And that night she slept, exhausted by it all, by the endless days of thinking, the endless nights of hoping.

It was that night that her son appeared in her dream, not a grotesque facsimile of Andy as in past dreams, but the perfect face of Andy, with all the lightness and clarity of his soul surrounding him as he walked out of what seemed like a foggy mist. She was sitting on the top of a hill for some reason, and out of this cloud appeared Andy, fresh as the morning sun, not a care in the world written on his face. Walking so calmly toward her, that wide smile lighting up the sky it seemed. He walked right toward her and paused, looking her right in the eye. Then he bent down on one crooked knee, grabbed one of her hands in his and said to her, "I'm fine, Mom. I'll be fine. There is no more pain anymore. I'm in a good place and you don't have to worry about me anymore, do you understand?" She started to cry in the dream, but he put his hand on her face, much like Delores had placed her hand on Ricky's face that same evening. And Andy said, "Don't cry for me, Mom. I'm all right." She stopped crying then and stared at him, her beautiful boy. For a second there was a flash of a body—his body—lying motionless in a field, eyes closed, arms lying beside him, his rifle laying on the hard dirt beside him. The image passed and it was Andy again. He nodded at her, smiling, then got up, turned and walked back to the cloud. He moved calmly into it and disappeared.

At that instant she awoke and felt a presence in the room. She looked around in the dark and seemed to see tiny lights. Or was she just imagining it? Imagining that the spirit of her son was there with her now, trying to console her, to make her feel at peace. And, oddly, she did feel better somehow. The pit of emptiness, of the unknown, of trying to understand it had been replaced, it seemed, with a calmness. Like the waves of the ocean washing gently upon the shores of time.

The next morning she got out of bed and felt different.
She was sitting on her porch, looking out at the day, waiting for him. And at ten to nine in the morning, Sergeant Young appeared right on schedule, pulling his car up to the curb, shutting his door softly, and walking toward the house, jaw set, to give her the news, the news she already knew.

An hour later, the Sergeant long gone, there was another knock on the door. Delores wiped her eyes, and got off the couch where she lay. When she opened the door, a young cub scout was standing there with bags of caramel corn to sell. She smiled at him as he said his name—Matthew Stevens—gave his learned spiel about raising money for the troop. "Okay," she said. "I'll take two, no wait...give me three."

"That'll be six dollars," the boy said.

"Oh, wait," Delores said. "I left my money upstairs. Can you wait for me for a second?" The little brown haired boy nodded. She invited him into the foyer, then ran upstairs to the boys' room.

When she came back down she said, "Oh, there's my purse," as if she had forgotten it, headed for the living room and pulled a five and a one out of her wallet. Then she walked toward the boy and handed him the money. He handed her the plastic wrapped bags of caramel corn. Then she pulled out the thing she held behind her back, and handed it to the boy.

"Umm, we generally only accept money, M'am."

"No, you don't understand," she said, this is for you. I want you to have it. It's very special. It was my son's. He was a Cub Scout, too, but he would want you to have it now."

"Well," he said looking down at the baseball mitt, putting it on his hand and pounding it lightly with his fist, "if you really think it's all right. . ."

She reached over and brushed the boy's hair out of his face quickly, and looked deep into his eyes. "I know it's all right, Matthew. Just think of it as a present from Andy."

"Andy?"

"Andy was my son."

"Thanks, M'am. It's a beautiful mitt." He smiled, picked up his bag with his other hand and walked back down the walk, looking back at Delores, the mitt under his arm, and waved.

Delores smiled at the boy and waved back. In a moment, she thought, he would be walking down the street, out of sight, gone, gone forever.

Jill Battson

The Stone House

House whose walls are cut from the crust of the earth
pre-cambrian shield ossuary for farmers
resurrected from the tatters of neglect
you were built on the quiet land before
cars made distances nothing
your stones worn soft by prevailing winds
darkened to ochre and charcoal by rain
catching a glimpse of your welcoming lights
when walking the fields
on drizzle darkening autumn evenings
or your grey-yellow stones through
summer's heavy trees
means the house forms its word
around a meaning of home
blissful centering that promises belonging
house that will soothe city-tense psyche
shield me from the larger world
here is a softness that protects
small light and quietness in winter
cool breezes and gentle scents in summer
house, you are rock risen and hewn
older than time shaped
in the cradle of your history I have found my home.

Jill Battson

Beauty Mark

Beautiful, I am harboured in your body
meld myself with your connective tissue
blush at each move and stretch
the unseen brand of your lovemaking
I move downwards into your body
mark your wet membranes
with the badge of my progression
my cancerous bruises florid and unseen
as I proliferate noiselessly
when I break for air, surfacing on your ankle
I give you my flower
    moi fleur de mal
first a rose blush, flattened on the skin
then quickly, as I proffer my beauty,
a raised eruption, purple as royalty
sometimes my beauty mark
 beads blood jewels
sacrament of my adoration
      lacrimosa, lacrimosa, lacrimosa
by the time you notice me
I am already languishing in the warm moisture
of your lungs and gut
ridging the roof of your mouth with burgundy bubbles
I mark you for others' judgment
look at us, we are beautiful.

Jill Battson

Morgan's Bones

   — for Frank Morgan

When Frank's music envelopes me
in 7am rising light, the Chamisa blooming in my breathing
I am driving up through mountains, along the high road past Chimayo
carried away with the salty extravagance of sound
the smooth quality of knowing one's heart
remembrance of love lost and regained
a floating cushion of familiarity
and Frank's notes breathing across a landscape serene

the modulated security of distance

When Frank says
    put something of you in the place
he plunged me into a rest-of-the-day funk
like I could never be the jazz-loosened loose-bone thing he is
the improv that jazz is all about
a conversation that moves across the stage
lightening moments between the instruments
as the response is rethought
the voice that jazz speaks, Frank,
    tell me in that voice

When Frank plays his horn
it's like yesterday never happened
or tomorrow doesn't need thinking about
the music is just there, his breath following the voice
toffee skin, the reed leaning bottom teeth
his fingers squeezing the notes
melody he sees on his darkened retina
like nothing written and everything felt

when Frank says
    Always leave room to do what's in your heart
I feel squeezed like an exhalation of breath
like I cannot do what he does
even with my words

When Frank plays live
I hear the breathy intake of air beneath the music
the tack of saliva between tongue and reed
a cushioned tap of brass keys
I am hearing a life lived, a man learning
I am hearing Bird and Miles and Louis
remembering Thelonius with his wife packing a cardboard suitcase
in countless hotel rooms and back alleys, the weed urine aroma
Frank's history in the metallic edge of methadone
then I know it's too late for me to live that life

Melissa Studdard

Poem for the Women of Atenco, Mexico

with thanks to Lorian Hemingway,
champion of human rights

Take it now, this metaphor, your bread.
You've seen God bleeding in the streets
But the militia couldn't help, sooty faced
Themselves, disoriented by the shrapnel
Lodged beneath their right to choose
A peaceful life. Take these words flowing
Like wine. Let them salve where hands
Gripped too tight, where teeth broke the skin,

Where fists beat your notions of freedom
And equality flat as powdered dough, flat
As grapes crushed beneath the pointed
Boots of war. Let these words recall
Those things you meant to be before
Rage came storming through your town.
Let these words be your appetizers,
Served to you with humility and respect,
That which you were denied four years ago.
Let these words be your dinners and your desserts,
Evidence that you are being heard. Eat them
 Proudly and let them sustain you, even
As the others sip margaritas on the patio,
Even as the others go on about their lives
Oblivious to what you have endured. Your time
Will come. So keep your aprons on, women
Of Atenco; keep your eyes on the timer
And your hearts on the cause—because grapes
Beneath the feet will become wine, and
Dough that is set aside will rise. Yes—
That neglected, resilient dough will rise.

Melissa Studdard

Om

He sent us flowers without a card,
God did—that trickster soul.
It must have been a sound that started it all,
And he's still out there somewhere, laughing
While we seek directions, or direction,
While we, the addressees, search for an addresser,
While we sort and sift and categorize and collect,
Divide, classify and analyze. Our refrigerators hum to us,
And heaven knows the bugs make their merry at night.
 Once I even saw the color yellow hum
When I imagined van Gogh stroking its thick,
Vibrant passion onto the page.
That yellow song was anything but hum drum.
I swear, I felt it on the roof of my mouth
And at the back of my throat
Like a yogic ritual or some sort of Tantric stunt.
Even deep in my chest, yes, I felt the hum.
And in the other room—the clothes in the washer,
Round and around they went, their own spinning universe,
And next to them, a parallel world, the dryer,
Connected to the same outlet,
Hum, hum, humming away.
This life is anything but ho hum,
With all this motion and noise.
Hell, I can hardly even hear over the hum of my phone,
Which I have cursed for interference,
Which I have indignantly labeled, "that silver piece of shit,"
Which I have threatened to replace (like it cares),
And which was really Om all along.
Washing clothes, I've since learned, is an act of prayer.

Melissa Studdard

Poet

Now you yourself are a tabula rasa,
the stark, blank page your fellow in emptiness
the lovely, blank page your window to the all.
You see through gauzy, windblown curtains:
flashes of light— the dancing rays spun
round a spinning girl, beneath the Asian pears,
beneath the ruby throated chirps of birds,
and you are her, and she becomes you.
Possibility glistens in the air like morning dew,
and even the humble ant dreams of sugar
lined trails as your senses flood with birdsong
and light. You can hardly tell which is which,
which comes from the bird and which
from the sun as synaesthesia engulfs you
like a hungry mood, and you begin to understand
why Thoreau wanted to devour the woodchuck raw,
to drive his teeth into the beating pulse
of nature itself. Only you don't want
to eat the bird at all, but, rather, her song,
and to sit as near as possible the open window,
to eat the rays of light too and consume the shimmering,
false distance between yourself and this world
so that you may be a conduit which brings
these lovely, pulsing wonders to the page
still breathing and throbbing with life.

Viola Weinberg

I Have Come to Beat the Drums

I have come to beat the drums
                     Of love

Because love is stronger than
                     Terror

And terror is worse than
                     Death

I have come to beat the drums
                     Of love

Because music is closer to God
                     Than gunfire

I am beating a drum because drums
                     Are heartbeats

And hearts need hope and hope needs
                     Memory

And memory is stronger than
                     Forgetting

And forgetting is worse than
                     Death

I am putting my hand on the skins
                     Of this drum

Because connection is more important than
                     Isolation

Because wounds do not heal without
                          Touch

And no matter how deep
                          Wounds must heal

Or nothing will live and living is stronger
                          Than death

And life is bravery and love is our
                          Liberator

Because love is a powerful agent of
                          Life

And life is fragile but the will is
                          Strong

And life is the ribbon that goes on and
                          On

I have come to beat the drums of
                          Love

Like rain beating a tin roof because
                          Life

Is a clatter and love is a messy, noisy
                          Song

And songs are closer to God than
                          Bombs

And love is the only answer to
                          Fear

And life cannot co-exist with
                          Fear

And life will not exist without
                             Love

And the drums of love are energy
                             And blood

And the drummer goes on and on and on
                             And life

Is the song of drums and love
                             Nourishes

And death cannot flourish until the song
                             Ends

And imagination is believing and life goes on
                             For memory

Is stronger than forgetting and
                             Remembering

Is the lyric of the spirit and peace
                             Peace

Is the answer to misery and grief and
                             Peace

Is the sound of a wound knitting and
                             Life

Is the song of wounds healing
                             And healing

Is believing that life goes on and the
                             Drum

Keeps the beat and love is a lamb
                             And love

Is the only hope we
                             Have.

Cynthia L. Bryant

Crossroads

Nightfall contained pitch-thick air of desert
though muted nightlights glistened above
no light made its way through the doorless opening
into the adobe pueblo with earthen floors
floors to sit, fitfully sleep upon
ample water from a nearby well

Daylight hours spent in town
daughter perched on hip
husband's eyes hawk-like from a distance
as we pulled manna from the hearts of tourists
for formula, diapers, food
enough to gas the psychedelic painted van
bartered for in Colorado the month before

Barely into my seventeenth-year
on the sly with Army-deserter husband
who hid beneath a dark-haired wig
tied with rawhide band at his forehead
Our hungry daughter
whose bottom prickled with rash
that year outside of Taos

Summer heat brought happy diversions
shared with brightly clad wanderers
whose long hair, beads, bandanas
colored my world
as they trickled eastward
toward rumors of days and nights
filled with free-love, music

We stayed on
unable to follow the dreamers

Our young family
pressed further into earth

that summer of '69
battling survival and dysentery
against colorless New Mexico backdrop
under shadow of fading youth

Cynthia L. Bryant

Panther

The stranger's open hands
found mine
grasped firm
pulling me up
on to the landing

Clothed in black
Leather pants
hung low
on narrow hips
encircled by ovals of silver

Long-sleeved shirt
hugged close to

masculine shoulders
several buttons left undone

Long restless curls
wandered his head
wild and free

Intense cat eyes
almost golden
gauged me with curiosity

Self-satisfied smile
on the prowl

> *Hey Honey*
> *What ya doin' here?*

Suddenly self-conscious

I mumbled something
about my old man

being in the opening band

    Too bad, he purred
showing me a chair

Later on my boyfriend and I
hand in hand
lost in a sea of faces
on darkened dance floor
One beam of light shone
on the promoter

    Time has come
    to welcome
    here from L.A.
    with their hit
    Light My Fire
    topping the charts
    let's hear it for
      The Doors

Drums thumped solitary
like a clap of thunder
Strobe lights flashed
As electric harpsichord played intro
my man in black

Skye Leslie

Come. Now.

Listen, I've no time any longer for long answers
and humming under the breath. I've gotten hold of some truths
and they are staples in my hands B nailing all the detritus to the wall
of my resignation.

This is the day, the time is now.
The words are redemption,
reconciliation and grace. Yours for the asking.

Come now, and we will tear the curtain of separation,
take the long walk to pools of recovery and there it is
we'll find all the sheared glass, torn tree limbs,
the sweat of our dreams and the gravel which was once our voices.

I'm telling you, it is possible to take up the dish thrown down
and use it for the paving of a bridge between mistaken identity
and the realization of our shared places on this earth. We can walk it.

As we remove the driven nail, the thorned crowns and turn water
into wine, we become partakers of a creation left in our hands,
performers of a magic exceeding the miracles left behind.

Listen, come now, I'm telling you this can be done
and now.

Jim Christy

Why We're in Afghanistan

Stevo cut down by small arms fire
And John fell into a well. Two Captains
Dead in one Afghanistan week
And "a major lost both his legs."

A piper of the Princess Pats
Played as their peers
Put them on the plane. And
A better ramp ceremony you
Never did see and you'll see
Plenty more.

But what of that major and his legs?
Where did he lose them? Or did
He step on a mine? The details
Don't matter only
That he lost them—

Doing his duty, that was.

Those fellows on the tarmac
All looked solemn, determined
And young. Maybe they'll live
To get stoned again
Come Saturday night, and even
Survive their tour, go back
To Creemore and Elkhorn
100 Mile House and Trois Riviere
Where they'll wake up some morning
A score and a half years from now
And wonder what the hell was
Going on in that godforsaken place
Over there when they were young.

Sure there're more than a few that
Made it, though some like Stevo
and Jon are dead but what about
The other fellow? Will he too always be,
Like the Brigadier General said, "In

The thoughts and prayers
Of the entire Canadian Task Force",
Or just "Old what was his name
That good looking fellow, >a major
Who lost both his legs.'"

Is he back home with a generous
Compensation package and a couple
Of belt on legs? Or maybe a rollerboard,
The plastic covered titanium, state
Of the art number that comes with
The lightweight rubber blocks B individually
Contoured to fit your hands B all
The better to push himself about
And slide underneath automobiles
And fix
The Universal problem.

Could be he's doing push ups
For beers right now in the pub
Back home. That girl he was

Slated to marry, is she
Still by his side, looking
Down on him?

Bet his legs even now are calling
Him but from heaven knows
Where. Are they with the Captain
Down at the bottom of the well?
Did someone throw them
To the dogs of Khandahar? Or

Did dusky kids play football
With his feet? Maybe they
Just up and walked away, his
Legs, over mountains
And through poppy fields
And are right now relaxing
In a room in Peshawar. Or

Maybe there're up in the sky,
And make constellations
Like a billion other limbs

From a million other wars.

Jim Christy

Lollygagging Moon

Balloon floats with brown leather
Feet on the zocalo. Inflatable television
Characters with ancient people
On a string.

Then in a puff of wind one woman
Rises from the cobblestones and
Soon is looking down on tingas
And chimichangas, Franny's bench
And Germans. High above hotel lobby
Folk dancing and out past city limits
Across Indian land toward a sky
Darker than mole sauce.

I can see Orion's Belt on Bob's
Sponge pants and a cat's paw
Cloud just missed good old Daffy
Duck to lie across
A lollygagging moon.

And the woman cuts her strings
To float free in the Azteca,
Zacateca, Iroquois, Chippewa,
Yaruma, Tarahumara
Taino, Arapahoe
Heavens
And see if
The moon's a balloon
And the Great Spirit but
A puff
Of wind.

Jim Christy

The Heart of the World

I'm on my way, happy
To be going again. Coming back
Maybe never. My passport pages
Are filled with all these
Pretty stamps and visas,
I've got no baggage
To check nor am I carrying on
Any preconceptions.
I do have, however, more dreams
Than can be stowed in the overhead
Compartment or under
The seat in front of me. Oh, I
Can go to Tiflis or, maybe,
Toronto; Hudson's Bay
Or Havana will do but what
I really want to find

Is the place that's not
In the seat pocket by my knees
Or on the map at the back
Of the airline magazine.
Maybe the flight attendant
Can be of assistance.
I press the button and the light
Goes on: "Sir/Madame
Help me, please. I am
Looking for the Heart
Of the World."

Wendy Babiak

Testament

I dreamed I returned
as a huge crow.

I asked the world to confess
its bitter flavor.

I asked the redwood to give witness
to the last 2,000 years.

In the trembling of its plenitude of leaves
I heard its answer:

The obscure past lies enfolded
in childhood's mists

too complicated to disclose. You
fly and see things

from the sky. Let the loss of green
speak for itself.

Wendy Babiak

Shivasana

I first thought to call this
Lying in Corpse Pose
but this is going to be a truthful poem
and nobody calls it that these days
Relaxation Pose more palatable
to we Westerners so afraid of Death
we'd rather deny its existence
than simply get used to the idea
or even embrace it. Shiva
is one of the old Indian gods
Lord of Death and Destruction
they say. Joined with Shakti
in an eternal dance
he ushers in creation
by making room.
Scavengers and decomposers
do his work. So do fire and flood.
His devotees smoke ganja, the herb
that frightens so many when they
seem to feel their breath
and their hearts in their chests
moving for the first time.
(Satish couldn't take it.
It took four med students at the party
to talk him out of his panic.
Even then he lay there
trembling like someone dying
waiting out the half life
of the cannabinoids
coursing through his blood.)
And sadhus plunge their arms
elbow deep into the ashes of the dead
then smear the oily smut

over their faces, on their bodies
going about Shiva's business
like dirty gray suits
reminding all who care to look
what waits for us at the end
of each of our stories. So
every yogi honors him
at the end of her practice
assuming the posture, flat on her back
incorporating into each nerve and muscle fiber
the energy manifested
letting what's been made loose
firm up in proper alignment
before moving into the work of the day.
Perfect stillness, except
the waves of the breath
rising and falling completely.
In such a state, breathing sometimes slows
so much that full moments pass
multiple heartbeats in stillness between
the end of an exhalation
and the downward pull of the diaphragm
beginning the next intake. It's then
my body remembers death
the lack of breath he found
while I danced my own dance with Shiva over there
just feet away from where my healthy body
relaxes now. Poor dear husband
come in quick at the sound
of the skullcrack of my collapse
brainstem shut off like the lights
when the bill's not paid. Later
he told me he stared long moments
into my open, vacant eyes
mourning me: no heartbeat
no movement of air
where he'd taken for granted
he'd find it for at least a few more decades.
Thank the gods for a doctor's instincts.

No, thank love for the unwillingness to let go.
Someday we'll have no choice. But while we can
we'll live every day fully
not ruled by Death like those who fear it
but grateful for every moment of life
letting each breath chime its thankful mantra:
Not yet.
Not yet.

Diana May-Waldman

If I were Rich, I would pay people to stop being assholes

We're traveling in different circles
traveling fast and nowhere
I don't want the glitz, the glamour
the accolades, atta boys,
pats on the a back
don't want the fame
don't want the money
no shiny cars
big rock diamonds
clicking of cameras
headline news
No, I don't want
to be a best seller
pretend I am Bukowski
making a living off
the word "fuck"

I just want a garden
to feed the world
want peace
and love and more love
never enough love
I want buckets of love
to spread around
want to pistol whip love
on baby killers, rapist,
wife beaters, kidnappers

No, I don't want the money
don't want to be rich
just want the power, power
to stop you.

Diana May-Waldman

I Am a Poet

I am a Poet
because I love words
and thoughts
because words
tangle in my mind
and smooth on paper
I am a Poet
because my father
was a Poet
and because
my mind wanders
and my fears rise like bath water
and sometimes
I am afraid
to feel.
I am a Poet
because I am defiant
made raw and real
by love and nature
and sometimes I hurt
until it festers
breaks loose
and because I love to lie
in my bed with papers and pens
nailing love cries to my heart
and because I sigh under
the baggage of the past
and I am a Poet because
I have lived with ice blue shackles
and the pink eggshells of anger
and it needs to be told
and because I can breed moods

dramatic and still
volatile with rage
and I am Poet
because I ache in secret
and heal out loud
I am a Poet because
German men
killed baby Jews
and left mothers
with drooping, aching, empty breasts
and I am a Poet
because someone killed
John Lennon
for the fame of a skeletal moment
and I am Poet
because death makes us
stupid with grief
and unbuttons vulnerability
making us cry glass tears
and I am a Poet
because women are
still ripped into sparks
and scattered like stale bread
and I am a Poet
because I feel terror
when I sleep
an insomniac woman
with a cottonmouth tongue
demanding to be heard and I am a Poet
because Sylvia Plath
stuck her head in an over
leaving babies with bread and jam
and because Anne Sexton
had more to say
and I am a Poet because
racism needs to be thrown off
like a cloak, holding our hearts
and because
bombs explode and planes crash

and young boys are buried
with American flags
and the world is still in secondary love
I am a Poet because babies are thrown in
trash cans, left in bathrooms
because someone wished they
were someone else
and because people are hungry
while others with meat cutting knives
stab into human flesh
and because there is no apology
for smoke billowing factories
spreading poison on playgrounds
where children laugh in homeboy style
and 30 years later, die stiff lunged
and I am a Poet, because
homophobes hide behind velvet hats
pressing hatred against their lips
and the white crusted mouth sores
of A.I.D.S., seal bodies in polished oak
and we make quilts to remember
the silent sleepers
and because
even though this world
can be dangerous
and unforgiving,
offensive and frantic,
I still believe
still believe in you
and still believe in me
I still believe in love.

David LaBounty

the even keel
(another poem for Raymond Carver)

bonded by alcohol
& a common culture
he says that you
should be happy now, now

that your life
is on track &
on an even keel

you nod your
head slowly, long
for the cigarettes
that you gave
up a dozen years
ago during those
dying stormy days
of arguments &
 slamming doors &
driving penniless
across half the country

you say it's all a matter of taste

what would one rather do?
you ask out loud

sit along the banks

of a still & stagnant pond
or sit on the beach

of just about any coast

watching the waves

crash into the surf

the shore birds
dancing across
the sky

not quite touching the face of heaven.

David LaBounty

at the college bookstore

there are
too many
pretty girls
with thawed
faces that
I will freeze
that way

forever

& me so
out of tune
signing
not too many

I am not,
the bull in the china shop
not even,
the poet dying on the vine
I am only
the crack in the culture

a
crack starting
to

disappear
&

die

David LaBounty

six lanes of mercy

today

this morning

an 8 point buck,

the kind hunters
drool over
got hit
by a car
in front
of my shop

my shop
along a

decaying

suburban
thoroughfare

six lanes wide

lined with

strip malls

repair shops

& the

mouths of

subdivisions

like so many

gap-toothed

aluminum sided
smiles

the deer wasn't

dead but it

couldn't walk

& it tried

so very hard to

get up &

walk but

all it could

do was drag
its hind along

the potholed

asphalt

traffic stopped

people gathered

motorists in

ball caps &

pick up trucks
 yelled put

it out of its

misery as

if those of

us standing

there knew

what to do

about misery

the police

came in
2 cars &

debated

for a moment

one cop

pulled on

his black

gloves &

drew his

black 9mm

out of its
holster

he squatted

next to

the deer &

fired a

shot clean

& true

right through

the temple

blood came

out the other

side & the

deer nodded

itself so

very gently

off to death

the cops approached

they patted the

deer &

said something

about processing

it, something

about firm

hindquarters

& venison steak

& I realized

that's what

meat is

meat is

misery &

suffering

meat is the

calf cut at

the neck

while hanging

upside down

in a slaughterhouse row

meat is the

pale thin

boy on

the playground

picked last

when choosing

up sides

meat is the

young soldier
stepping
off a

one-way plane

meat is the

reluctant

bride the

day & years

after her

honeymoon

meat is the

drunk & lonely

man spending

hours on

the internet

surfing porn

while trying

to find the

perfect match

for his

would-be orgasm

meat is the

Alzheimer's

patient on

the special

floor of a

nursing home,

the patient

whose name

is on so many

insurance claim forms

meat is me

or maybe even

you driving

to work in

the morning

just to spend hours

chained to a desk

or factory floor

watching the

clock tick
reluctantly by

which is just to say

meat isn't always

food or even death

meat is also life, as

meat just simply is.

Harris Schiff

Double Cross

So

within

another continent

another culture

cheap

petty

old

both of us

hanging in at 20 Euros a day

then back into the Divided States until the hurricanes end

if they end

My respects to all

insane

hooked on petro
There is supposedly a prototype fusion reactor here
It's just a boondoggle
a scam

nothing but a huge
flat

hundred million dollar construction site where
theoretically
something will be built
someday

The banks are structures of abuse
continuing to absorb
the Wealth of Nations
to our great distress

A vital trick would be
utilitize the Energy Conglomerates
and send the profits to everyone on earth

But Aristocracy is Real
has been here millennia

in castles, minarets, temples, churches, tents, mansions, caves

doesn't give a crap about mother
or child

Right Sir?

invisible
funds

Fun

"enchanté" (a pleasure to meet you)

desoleé (I'm sorry)

The Job

is an obsolete concept

Something Must Change

will change

violence ongoing and done

we

victims trapped in

self-perpetuation

Our earth erupting

shaking off the virus

us

*　　*　　*　　*

heart

hear

Here

Listen

Soul Swings

TURN THE VOLUME UP

WAY UP

*　　*　　*　　*

Ah beloved victim you appear insane
beyond any ability to stop

to heal

so sexy
so sad
so beautiful

So much work raising the kids

to breathe these poisons

Drunk

Stoned

Cluelessly pursuing a future

an unlikely probability construct

The Fed feeds you lies

Pray or Prey

Pay or go

*   *   *   *

I'm in the boat

moving with the currents

Thank you!

*   *   *   *

Refuse to be hopeless

Refuse to cooperate!

Learn Esperanto!

Godspeed!

Good Luck!

Harris Schiff

Second Honeymoon

Disco jazz is an old song now
disappearing time makes new
sleek jet projectiles soaring above
Manhattan spires
reaching up into haze

here comes another one

an arc of spume
a mound of brick

Jordan Zinovich

Back in the Bus

Josélene is moonlight
imagined by love note
in wild rhythm counterpoint.

The child on her counterpane
calls to her girlhood
with light conversation—

Recalling a long ride
through bright winter nighttime.
That stranger encounter

Remembered as kindness
and treasured in silence

through uncounted years,

When pale freckles dusting
the lines of a smile
calmed a deep terror awhile.

Jordan Zinovich

Reminiscence—One

> (in the style of L.C. for Adele)

I once had three young lovers:
Cherry picker, Coxswain, and John.
The three all came together
when last I tried this on.

I tailor words to clothe you,
standing naked to myself,
but neither of us cleans up true
in sickness or in wealth.

I write this to remind me
not of the loves I had,
but of the love that's stayed with me
through good times and through bad.

Jordan Zinovich

Logorrhea

    You trusted the woolly spirit; lived on a shoestring (which wasn't very nourishing); all for none you stumbled on. Whatever can a city state of artless loss—minimalism more majestic than lost soul music masters slaving to save (only to spend a borrower be) in green as mescaline—cause no one wins by whining why! Why? Why not claw sideways, seaways to be silent where the bee sucks suckers born instants before minutes that reverse. Imagine otherwisdoms otherwheres blankly on the spot—Out! Says Jain to prick: Out! Out dumbed Spot.
    In other words: Lighten up! Grab a reel!
    Glow gaseous as airhead ruminants grinding lumpmeal; gnoshing Gnostic familiarities holus bolus. Growl by gulps and farts to the heart of things; probe as deeply as the nautilus would could it clearly recall all forty thousand big league sweeps for the starveling intelligent life near Uranus—I know that butt. What is one man, facing such sudden profound inanity?
    A bit of advice: If the foo shits, kiss cranny goodbye.

Angel Caywood Lambert

fear

it doesn't simply look upon you with adoring eyes and lust
it wants you
it will stop at nothing to get you
it will court you with pretty phrases
give you compliments
make you king
it will set you high
then knock you off just to watch you fall
it will make you feel strong
knowing that you can't win in your weakness
it will drain all the energy you would have used for other things
and render you useless
until you give in and use the power it makes you think you have
it wills your mind with memories not yet made
fooling you into believing lies
but these are lies that you need to survive
without them you can't even breathe
it takes all your hopes and dreams and all your success
and it waits until you are about to win
because it knows you need it for strength
without it you can't stand
and just when you cave in and reach for the strength you think it holds
it lets you fall
and laughs
because you helped it make you fail.

Angel Caywood Lambert

Ribbons

cut me into ribbons
then tie me in your hair
take away my mirror
yet reflect me everywhere
lie to me until your own heart
forgets what you feel
sugarcoat your love for me
then tell me that it's real
cut me into ribbons
then tie me in your hair
take away my mirror
yet reflect me everywhere
lie to me until your own heart
forgets what you feel
sugarcoat your love for me
then tell me that it's real

John Roche

Before May Day, 1971

Two weeks in tent city
West Potomac Park
demos everyday
building towards May Third actions:
"Bring the War Home"
"If the Government won't stop the war,
we'll stop the Government."

We give visiting Massachusetts Congressman a pipe when he visits
our affinity group's tent; he puts it to his lips but doesn't inhale; a
coupla wks earlier, on school trip to DC, I'd smoked dope with John
Kerry's vets on the Mall, the day after they threw their medals over
the White House fence

Chill April night
vats of hot marijuana tea
courtesy of the Hog Farm
I partake but skip the soup & brown rice line
to crowd onto dilapidated bus
(Gray like the police bus I'll ride soon enough)
to Seatrain concert
at elegant old theater
 (Free tickets for the ragged Freak Brigade)

Balcony seat, but with the tea's effects
I prefer floor
Looking up
to watch the rococo ceiling fresco jump
to the fiddle's anarchic orders

John Roche

Pit Stop, '71

Pike's Peak of Reader's Digests
I leaf through every page of every issue
during that weekend in Colorado Springs county lock up
there for hitchhiking with no ID—
gave my name as Joseph Hillstrom.

Time stretched out like a stack of dental hygiene magazines
browsed while waiting for a root canal
and three days would have been thirty
 but for kindness of strangers
—two of Dorothy Day's disciples—
who paid my fine
and I thank them to this day.

The Reader's Digests proved indigestible
So I shat them out
then said farewell to the great state of Colorado
and hello to New Mexico—
because I wouldn't be caught dead in Utah.

John Roche

City of Gold (The Best Ride Ever), 1975

Leaving Las Vegas (lost a buck fifty to the slots)
forced to sleep in the desert, watching for scorpions and snakes
it gets hot early, then by noon hotter still
Six or seven others visible up the line
their thumbs jutting out

About to give up hope
when Winnebago appears
stops repeatedly
picks us all up
gives each one a cold Coors
says, We're heading for the brewery
in Golden, Colorado
so sit back and enjoy the ride!

Donald R. Carson, Sr.

Indian Mind

This was my land, that we did vow
to plant the fruit, the fields to plow
This was my land, forever to stay
until you came with your fire sticks to drive us away.

You killed our braves, women and child
We were treated like animals
with your minds gone wild.

You took our land,
gathering up our hands,
tied in a bind
but you can never have
an Indian's mind.

Donald R. Carson, Sr.

Two Different Worlds in War

Come and stand by me, my brother
You wear a star
I wear a cross
The love of one another
can't be lost.
Come and stand by me, my brother
Take my hand, in a stand
side by side
fight until foes
have given up
Come my brother, let us pray
pray, to see another day.
Come my brother
let's walk away
to old to fight these wars
Come my brother, let's walk away
we've been brave and true
let's walk away brother, a Christian and Jew.

Ars Moriendi

On Religion and Oil

You can not have me anymore
I will not be your spiritual whore
You can not come and take my life
Not because I am a wife
Not because I am a mother
But because I belong to another
You can not have me anymore
I will not be your ritual whore

Ars Moriendi

On Yoko and The Peace of John Lennon

I saw a woman holding on to all that she had
Her words ran out like assassination
How far must we have gone
When did peace need mediation
You can not silence it with a gun
Once it has already touched a nation

John Burroughs

John Cage Engaged and Uncaged

Sunken funkin' telepumpkin
Tell a country bumpkin who I am
And then let him tell you.

Both will tell it true
Though their perspectives
Seem contradictory
I'm born of hickory
And rectory
Blind Bartimaeus and
Insightful inspectory
True tale and muddled myth
On an identical trajectory.

John Cage
Or someone like him
(is anyone like anyone
more than anyone is unlike?)

Said disharmony
Does not exist
And the peaceniks are pissed.

Corn isn't hominy
But hominy is corn
And care isn't clothing
Though care can be worn
And all can be born
And all can be torn
And loved and forlorn
And warned and scorned
And according to some bother
Or brother or other

Reborn.

Sunken funkin' telepumpkin
Born of a couch potato
And a pureed tomato
An almost dead and
Buried berater

Blind hate hater
Lover
Elater
Thin ice skater
War abhorrer
Saint and horror
Mental (and governmental)
Master baiter
And sooner or later
Repeat reincarnator.

I am a living death
An awakened dream
Ash unconsumed
And a silent scream
Reconcilable
So called contradiction
And factual fiction

John Cage
Uncaged

Inadequately aged and yet
Timeless
A sublime mess
Subconsciously clothed and
Consciously undressed
Said worse and better are no less than best
Corn is hominy
And there is no disharmony
Only harmonies

To which our ears (my dears)
And our fears
Are unaccustomed.

John Burroughs

Bloodshot

Indian summer sun squints, bloodshot like the
Wide wounded eyes of my cynical Seneca ancestors.
On and on
   and anon,
An endless queue of unrelenting conquistadors,
Lusting for booty
   or bust,
Defile our trust and defame the name of God
   in the name of God.
Opportunity does not knock for trusting tribesmen,
  be they from Arizona
  Africa
  the Amazon
    or Akron.
Riding roughshod over every allegedly endless empire
Including America the beautifully dutiful,
The cursed hearse of history leads a parade of pathetic
  and unsympathetic plotters,
  plodders,
  priests and presidents,
Electable eels who feel their forked tongues
  and dung
Make them agents of distinction
  instead of
    extinction.
Sweetly sighing lullabies of liberty
  and expediency,
These leaders open
Their bomb bays
  as they pray
First for the unconditional surrender of their enemies
And last,
  if at all,

For the bloodshot souls
Of the soon to be charred
Children of Hiroshima
   Hanoi
   Belfast
   Belgrade
   Baghdad
   Bethlehem
Coming soon
   to a theatre
   of war
   near
   you

John Burroughs

Square

Television, no
please, tell a vision instead—

Turn off and turn on.

Dianne Borsenik

Conscientious Objector

Don't want to be put in a you-niform.

Don't want to be marshalled into you-nity.
Don't want to be assimilated into the rank and file,
marched along smartly,
don't want to be dog-tagged and ten-miled.
Don't want to be ordered and orderly,
don't want the corners
of my blanket tucked,
bed made up tight as a drumhead.
Don't want to be boxed in,
forced to fit, all straight line and eyes forward,
pushed up and put down.
No rattatattat for me.

My music billows.
It waltzes and tarantelles
like a dervish
in psychedelic estrus,
it harpsichords and theremins
in unearthly scales.
My music rolls on the floor with impossible
abandon, hangs inverted from the pole,

defies gravity,
does wild splits,
gets down and dirty.
My music jumps way out of line, gives authority
the finger, swears in another language.

My music won't be quarantined.
It ripples and radiates like a fifty five kiloton
atomic virus, flashes
flowerchild peace signs

in all directions. It positions daisies
in the bore holes of rifles,
drapes lovebeads on strands of razor wire,
backpacks into the wilderness
wearing only a smile.
It uncages all the animals.
It smears lipstick on your collar.

My music says no as much as it says yes.

Don't want to be put into a you-niform.

Don't want to be marshalled into you-nity.
The general idea is this, man:

I don't want to be all I can be.
I want to be all that I am.

Dianne Borsenik

Fire Burn and Caldron Bubble Tea

Fair-haired children play
at war; adults don't have franchise
on getting even. Phalanxes of young
minds have crushed revolutions,
shaped them into tapioca beads
that get stuck in the straws
of lamely manufactured peace.
Only the strongest dreamers will survive.
Memorize your way
out of this black maze; recognize
the Minotaur's minions by the fruits
of their labors. Drugged and drowsy,
playpen nations find complacency
in the blood they tap and drink.
Children of Jupiter melt
snowmen and snowwomen alike
with their lightning bolts, hurl foul
epithets at diplomacy, brush the ashes
of history from shoulder and thigh.

Dianne Borsenik

Lovechild

make incense from the flowers
dance naked in the light
weave a blanket
fringed with stars
to cover you at night
breathe kisses to the morning
braid songs into your hair
blow wishes on
the feathered spores
that surf the curls of air
and if a storm should hurt you
pour honey on the pain
chase the clouds
and catch them
then laugh
and drink the rain

.

William Page

Ballad

Two sparrows built their nest
in my thoughts this spring.

Little lovers, I asked,
has the forest become
so desolate and bare
that you cannot find
a tree for your nest?
Is there no stout oak
or budding maple
where you would rather sing?

"The winter was long,"
they chirped, as they jumped
and flew among my thoughts,
"and the trees are black
and dressed in ash this year.

But your thoughts are strong
and pliant and complex.
Look how easily
a strand of dried grass
and a little mud
is perched and held
among the tender
branches in your mind."

An army passed through
our country last fall.
Is it not terrible?
Do you not hate the greed
of the men who burnt
the trees that are your home?

Do you not blame mankind?

"Blame? We cannot blame.
We will build our home
among your ideas.
What is terrible in that?

There are two suns among
your thoughts and a moon
that is always full.
What is terrible in that?
We do not know hate.
Is it like the cat?
Can it climb trees?
Does it kill? Is it alive?"

It cannot climb trees,
but it does kill.
I have cut it from
my thoughts many times,
but its roots are deep
and hard to dig out.
Look, the stones at the
bottom of my mind
are hard and far down.
If an egg were to fall
I cannot imagine
how it would survive.

"Why are you worried?
Why should an egg fall?
Our nest will be strong
and plenty large enough.
Leave us your best thoughts
and come back in a month,
and we will be teaching
our fledglings to fly."

So I left my thoughts

and wandered among
the burnt trees and up
a deserted road.
That spring I lived
in a abandoned barn
with a speckled mare
and a black he goat.
We understood each other
perfectly. I fed them
as if they were human,
and learned about life

without thinking.
When I returned to
to collect the thoughts
I had left behind,
the nest was abandoned
and the sparrows were gone.
By then it was already
far into July.

Merrit Malloy

Choices

All you have to do
 to change your life
is to change your mind
... It really is that simple
But it isn't always
easy.

All you have to do to
stop feeling bad
is to start feeling good...but

'Feeling good' is not a
onetime event
It is decision we make
minute by minute
day by day
... It is a creation

The way to change the world
is to change your attitude
towards it
... not just once
but all the time.

Merrit Malloy

The Working Man

He worries a lot about income
as though money had anything to do with poverty
as though dollars would heal him
where he was poor.

He says he's working for his children
but his work prevents him from being with them
and he can't figure out why
they're not grateful

He used to talk about it
when he could still feel
back before the selfishness made thieves
of everyone...And now

He's afraid that he might die
so he's killing himself at work
and just to be safe (in case he doesn't)

He keeps a woman on the side...So
He's halfway here and halfway there and
always halfway ... So

He worries a lot about money
as though cash had anything to do with income
He leaves his family to surrogate arms and fast food

He's proud that he never cheats in business
and God knows he's loyal
The question is to whom?

It's a real talent to succeed
without getting
a head.

Diana May-Waldman

Penis

I want a penis
I want to give birth to it
so I can teach it to be nice
Teach it to be gentle,
teach it how to love.
I want it to ejaculate itself on the floor
spread it into the wood
and teach it how to be perfect history
without war or bloody hands,
I want to wash it, dry it,
hang it out to dry on a sunny day.
I want to set it on the window sill
have it look out at the flowers,
look to the sky and listen to the sound
of a child's laughter.
I want to introduce it to my friends,
have them pet it nicely, never being afraid.

I want my penis to feel the tears of women
and understand the animal cruelty of its nature.
I want my penis to be deaf, never listening
to the voices that define what it means to be a man.

Diana May-Waldman

Baby Jew

Words bite into me
hard on my flesh
leaving a bloody imprint
like still-life photos
the click of a button
and babies suck
on strange mothers
with nipples of guilt
trying to survive
twice the child
before and after
and men walk by
skin sagging
like ragged clothes
faded yellow stars of David
and the babies
pile up like dirty dolls
with lips still puckered
tongues curled
and clenched baby fists.

Michelle Dawson

River Time

River time
touches of sun
river runs
at the edge
trees sway
falling leaves
broken branches
float away
silent times
truthful days
side by side
standing tall
mesmerized
silent movement
peaceful times
dusk to dark
absolute love
forgotten times
hand in hand
forgiven choices
day by day.

Wrong Place / Wrong Time

Bill Harrison

Zip

Zip sat by the river, near one of his half dozen or so little hideouts spread over the nine-hundred-acre parcel of land where he served as care-taker/security guard. He often thought, Guard what, nine hundred acres of swamp, abandoned gravel pits and woods, a nice cabin that was empty fifty weeks of the year?

The owner, some rich dude from New Orleans only came there for two weeks of hunting deer in November each year. One week by himself. The next, a select few of his business partners. They drank, told lies and sometimes brought in hookers from New Orleans. Occasionally one of them might actually hunt. The other fifty weeks belonged to Zip.

He was paid well to cut grass, feed deer, kill wild hogs and maintain the big cabin. He had a small one bedroom cabin of his own, set near the entrance gate of the property and overlooking the East Pearl River, near the interstate and the railroad.

Zip's job gave him plenty of free time to hunt and fish, hang out with his friends get high, whatever he wanted. The check came every week and the owner liked him mainly because Zip kept his mouth shut, did his job and did it well.

Occasionally Zip would be called in to clean up things of an illegal nature. Zip had no problem with this. He had served two tours in Viet Nam. A dead person was just that. Dead. And they made good food for the gators, "His Babies" as he called them. Three twelve footers in the old abandoned gravel pit and plenty of young ones up and down the river. But the big ones were his pride and joy and his secrets.

The boss had an "I don't care to know, just handle it" policy and Zip handled it well.

For the past six months things had been quiet. The boss, not any of his partners had made any screw ups to be fixed and Zip enjoyed his quiet time and solitude.

Zip had a small group of young friends that had no idea of his secret swamp life. They did not know of his "Babies" or the service they provided. All they knew was that Zip was a cool older guy that had some money and didn't mind sharing his dope or his time. Anyone need anything, ol' Zip was there! Help with your car, a ride to work, borrow twenty or thirty dollars here or there was never a problem.

But Zip was a complex person. He always made it clear: If you borrow, pay it back. A favor was just that! A favor with nothing expected in return. Every one in the small circle respected him and his ways and he in turn respected them. He never made any passes at the women. He treated them all as ladies. Most were young enough to be his daughters.

One night a young stranger at one of the "Gatherings" made the remark, "Zip, dude, I ain't never seen you out with a chick. You ain't gay or something, are you?"

Zip smiled his smile and quietly replied, "I don't chase, I wait. I don't lust, I trust. There is no desire without love. I am a man, not a boy! I play no games, I take no names and in this rhyme did you find the answer to your question that will never be asked again?"

You could have cut the silence with an axe. Needless to say that guy never wanted to hang out again. Zip was a private, no kiss and tell kinda guy and we respected that.

It was an unspoken rule, you never went to Zip's place unless you were invited. Plus he would unlock the gate to let you in, lock you in, walk or drive you back when you were ready, or able, to leave. Another rule at Zip's: No one dries away drunk. Actually a good rule. Ninety percent of the time if you called he would invite you over or would politely say he was in the woods and would call you later.

Zip loved that damn cell phone. Always kept it on vibrate. Didn't want anything to break the silence or disturb the animals wherever he was out on the land, and he never missed a call.

There were times he would call one of us and simply say, "Gonna be gone for a few days or longer. Pass the word around. No calls till I get I get back. I'll let you know when I'm back."

And we wouldn't see him for a few days or weeks, but then one day out of the blue the phone would ring or he'd pull up in your driveway.

"Pass the word. I'm back and wanna have some fun." He'd laugh and for the close few it would be a good time.

Zip seemed to be particularly close to one of the girls in the group. A young single mother who had had her share of bad luck. He would smile and say, "We're just good friends." But you could see in his eyes, in his heart there was love. Behind his cold eyes there was a need. But Zip was Zip and he would never step over the line he himself had drawn. But there was no doubt he would kill anyone who harmed her!

* * * * *

The river flowed and Zip watched, he listened, he felt. His senses tingled. He had been out in the woods for three days. Maybe he would stay out two or three more. The weather had been great, spring turning to summer, no messes to clean up for quite a while. He had been reading many books on Native American philosophy, and begun to think differently about many things.

The silence helped, the flowing river helped. He was considering telling the boss to find himself another man, and moving up to Oregon or Washington state near his brother. But he loved this swamp, the warm weather almost year round and his "babies."

He thought silently of Angie and her young son. How he wished he was a younger man in a different time. How he wanted her to feel what he felt for her, but knowing it most probably would never be. He said a silent prayer for them and cast a handful of tobacco into the river.

"Carry my prayers to the sea, to Mother Earth and the Creator. Watch over this mother and child, protect them and all my young friends," he said silently as a single tear made its way down his cheek.

The gunshot broke the silence and the prayer.

"Fucking assholes," Zip cursed silently. Few people came this far up river this time of year and that's why he chose this spot this day. Then came the sound of the small boat motor. Some five hundred yards down the river he could barely make out the small narrow canoe with a small motor.

Zip took his high power field glasses out of his day pack. He focused in and could barely make out three forms in the boat. Coming up river against the current the canoe moved slowly. As the distance closed the gun barked again, echoing against the banks of the river and the over hanging trees.

"Redneck assholes," he thought as he watched through the glasses. The man in the front pitched a beer can in a high arch to the left of the canoe. Then the one in the rear raised a large handgun and fired a third volley. At about three hundred yards he could make out their faces. Dirty and unshaven, blue jeans, boots and light jackets, cammo ball caps. Standard issue for local rednecks.

It was the third party in the middle that drew his attention. Young blond female about thirteen years old. Adjusting the glasses tight to his face, she appeared listless, oblivious to the voices of the two men. The closer they came, the clearer their voices, the more pitiful her face bruised and bloody. Then the recognition.

The missing poster at all the local businesses. Missing: Melissa Baxter, age thirteen,

Poplarville, MS. Five foot, one hundred pounds, eyes: blue, hair: blond. Last seen at Picayune Movie Theater, a date three weeks old. Wearing blue jeans, tan shirt, black nylon jacket. Possible runaway, possible abduction. If seen, please call Pearl River County Police Department, blah, blah, blah.

Zip reached for the small cell phone in his pocket. He disliked the county police, but hated a child molester even more. In his haste the small phone slipped from his hand, down the embankment and lastly down to the catfish at the bottom of the river.

"Double fuck," he thought. The hideout was half a mile up river, too far to run and back. In it a scoped .22 magnum rifle and a hundred rounds. One hundred fifty yards now and slowing, he watched as his brain shifted into high gear.

"Remeaux Bayou, jus' up there," one said.

"I know where the hell I'm at you dumb fuck!" answered the pilot.

"Think we can get her to suck our peter again, Bro?" Front Man asked.

"Naw, Bro. She's all used up jus' like that other one. Besides, you knocked most of her teeth out yesterday. Might be a little rough on that little pecker of yours," he laughed.

"Shut the fuck up, Bro, or I'll—"

"You'll what, butt wipe?" the pilot said pointing the handgun.

"Aw, nuthin'. Less jus' finish this up and get back down river," answered Front Man.

Anger and adrenaline pumped through Zip like a 'hot shot' through a thoroughbred. With nothing but a hunting knife on his belt and a mind full of rage he started to move.

The canoe turned into a narrow cut on the opposite bank. Remeaux Bayou, a narrow deep canal that opened into a small lake, a snake infested, gator filled Hell!

"Dey was a big bull gator up here las' spring. Hope he's still here," said the pilot.

"Leave no evidence, that's what Pa used to say, right Bro?"

"Dats right, Bro," Pilot laughed, wiping his nose on his shirt sleeve.

"Cry fo' me some more, Little Miss Prissy Bitch," Front Man said as he slapped the child's hand. But her eyes could no longer make a tear. Her mind had gone to that special place, with no hope of returning.

Zip was in over drive, he had to reach her, had to do something to save her, had to try. Slipping into the cool swift river, he began to make his way to the other side. If he could cut them off, if he could take out the hand gun...

IF, IF, IF, too many IF's. His blood boiled and anger rose. The canoe was getting farther into the bayou. Zip pushed on through the marsh and snakes, a man possessed. Reaching a clear spot on the small lake, he drew a deep breath and cursed his luck. They had turned to the opposite end. Nothing he could do now but watch.

The Pilot, with a bit of hesitation or remorse, placed the hand gun at the back of the child's head and pulled the trigger.

Zip choked back a scream of rage. Through the field glasses the child's hopeless eyes met his before her head exploded.

"Gawd damn asshole! Ya got brain shit all over me man! Yous' suppose to warn me 'fore you did that," Front Man whined.

"Shut the fuck up and drop her over. We get back down river before dark, I'll buy you a beer," Pilot nonchalantly said.

Zip began to shake. The anger, the rage. The pleading in that child's eyes. He wanted to scream out. Then that calm, that peace that he had not felt since Viet Nam. A feeling inside that started in his gut like a shot of good whiskey with a cocaine chaser. Clarity. Vision. A task to complete. A mission. The child was dead: nothing would bring her back. Now as she slowly sank into the dark waters of Remeaux Bayou, he knew.

He would track them down, they would confess, then they would die!

* * * * *

The Ride

Wilmer and Clarence Vest, better known as Tater and Two Bit, sat at the small table in Sneaky's Bar, a small dive off Highway 90 near Pearlington, just off the highway and not far from the boat landing on the Pearl River. Tater, the eldest, sat silent sipping a Budweiser with a half pint of Jack Daniels sitting next to it. Two Bit was chattering away fueled with Southern Comfort and crystal meth.

The Vest brothers were social misfits. Rejects from society, they didn't fit in in any category. They weren't rednecks, stoners, nor could they be classified as citizens. Rejects summed it up best. Reared in the Honey Island Swamp on a house boat, they made their money fishing, trapping or stealing. Both had done time in both Mississippi and Louisiana. Brought up by a daddy that was far worse that either of them could ever hope to be.

PawPaw Vest had recently died in Angola Prison, serving a life sentence for the murder of a transvestite in New Orleans. Apparently he was too drunk to tell the difference between a he and a she until he woke up the next morning. Realizing what he had been to bed with, he then slit his throat and cut off his privates in a hung over rage.

"Two Bit, would you shut the fuck up. Your babbling too Goddamn much in public," Tator said quietly.

"Man I jus' can't keep from thinking about how good that last one was, man. But I want to pick the next one, man. You like 'em too young, man. They's tight, but theys got no titties, man, and I want one with some titties, man!"

"Two Bit. Last time. Shut the fuck up or it's lights out."

"OK, OK, Bro. Shuttin' up. Shuttin' up right now."

They were about to walk out when the sound of a Harley pulling in the parking lot made them stop and sit back down. Bikers loved meth and they had meth to sell. They had learned to cook from one of the Aryan Brothers in Angola Penitentiary, and had made good money at it since they were released two years earlier. There were plenty of good, secret spots in the Honey Island Swamp and the Vest brothers knew them all.

The biker walked in and slipped on to a stool at the bar. He ordered a Bud and nodded his head to the music from the Juke Box.

Tator and Two Bit were debating on approaching him first. Sizing him up, so to speak. Was he cool, was he a narc, or just another biker who knew of the little out of the way bar where you could get a cold beer and just about anything else you wanted?

The biker wasn't a big guy, sort of wiry about five ten to six foot. Long reddish hair pulled back in a pony tail, looked to be in his late forties to mid fifties. Tator poked Two Bit in his ribs and said, "He's a heap too damn skinny to be a cop."

The biker paid for his beer and motioned the barmaid closer, handed her a twenty whispering something to her. She smiled and nodded , "Yes!"

Tator and Two Bit watched as she walked to the door, hung the sign that said "Gone to Piss, Be Back in 15 Minutes" on the door, turned the lock and pulled the shade down on the front door.

Stormy the barmaid pretty much ruled the bar, did what she wanted, when she wanted and the owner didn't care. He rarely came in. The bar was just a tax write off.

Stormy was in her early forties, street smart and road weary, loved a free high and a good ride, on a Harley or in the sack. Apparently the biker had made a good offer!

Tater and Two Bit were surprised when she motioned them to the bar.

The bike dropped a small plastic baggie on the bar and said, "Cut us out four big ones, darlin'. I like good cold beer, pretty women and good company. This is the last of my shit. My cook got busted up north of Poplarville in the piney woods and I'm partying up what's left."

Stormy smiled a wide bright smile through parted red lips, thinking to herself she just might close early tonight.

Tater and Two Bit smiled quietly at each other thinking silently A new customer with money to spend.

Zip boiled inside. His plan and two weeks of tracking had finally paid off!

* * * * * *

The Plan

By the time Zip had reached the camp house, the small canoe was miles down the river. Cursing himself for not being prepared for anything, and vowing to himself that the child's death would not go unavenged, Zip sat down with pen and paper and laid out his plan.

1. Call the Boss, tell him he had a family emergency and would be gone for an undetermined amount of time.
2. Get his Harley out of storage, service it and start tracking.
3. Call up one of his young friends and purchase an ounce of crystal meth and a quantity of Roofies, a date rape knockout dope.
4. Get his gear ready for a road trip; a hunting expedition.
5. Pack up his two favorite hand guns, the heavy little 45/410 five shot revolver and the old Army Colt 45.
6. Start tracking.

With his list made he was in gear. No good plan worked without a list. He learned that in Nam. Zip followed his list step by step. After nearly two weeks of bar hopping, camping out, nonchalantly asking questions, tipping bar maids and buying drinks he found himself at the mouth of the Pearl River, in a bar, baiting two murdering pervert bastards.

"Lady, gentlemen I plan on getting' high and ride all the way to Pensacola, drinking, snorting, and fucking all the way!" Zip laughed.

"Here's to drinking," said Two Bit.

"Here's to snoring," said Tater.

"Here's to fucking!" laughed Stormy.

Stormy cut out four large lines, working the meth down to a fine powder with a credit card. Two Bit produced a cut down straw and the four of them passed it around.

Zip stashed the baggie back in his vest pocket, and the meth did its magic. The conversation rolled, everyone became barroom buddies. Stormy reopened the bar and moved seductively to the music on the juke box, smiling and winking at Zip every chance she could.

Zip would return her glances and gestures, considering her the Spoils of War.

Tater and Two Bit began to shoot a game of pool and talk between themselves.

Four customers came in, drank a beer or two then left. Around ten pm Zip touched his finger to his nose and Stormy hung the closed sign in the window. Zip dug out his baggie, handing it once again to the barmaid and held up four fingers. She pulled him close over the bar and kissed him, tongues exploring, heat building. Easing him back she said, "Wanna save some of that for later."

Zip smiled and pulled another baggie from another pocket, putting his finger to his lips in a shushing motion, an eye pointed to the Vest brothers. Stormy caught the message.

After they did another line Tater motioned for Zip to come sit at the table as Two Bit knocked the pool balls around the table.

"Dude, you said your cook just got busted," Tater spoke.

"That's it, man," Zip replied.

"Well, I just might know someone that can hook you up. You got a way I can get in touch?"

"No problem, man. Here's my number. Call ASAP. I got plenty of friends always looking, but it's just you and me, OK?"

Tater spoke quietly looking Zip in the eyes. "It's me and my brother there and you. You fuck me, you pay. You square, we're both money makers, straight up!"

"Straight up," Zip replied, handing him the phone number.

Stormy yelled out, "Closing time! Everybody out except you!" pointing to Zip. Everybody else left.

At sunrise as usual, Zip was up and ready to roll. Standing in the kitchen of the camper trailer behind the bar, Stormy's home away from homeless, she called it. The meth had worked its magic. He found who he had been tracking for two weeks. He also found something he had not expected; a lost soul with a good heart. They didn't just go straight from the bar and jump each others bones, but sat up for several hours talking. Stormy shared a life story of broken dreams and broken promises, and Zip gave her honest answers to honest questions. When the hour got late and the candles burned low the heat went up. And for the first time in a long time Zip didn't just fuck, he made love.

Stormy had shared with him that she was so thankful that he had come in the bar. She despised the Vest brothers. Fearful of them was the way she put it. Something about them reeked of death but she couldn't put her finger on it. She had said a few years back their daddy had tried to rape her one night after closing. He laid in wait for her behind the bar, grabbed her between the bar and camper. Her first though was robbery until he started to pull at her clothes. What he didn't expect was the sawed off twelve gauge she jammed in his crotch.

The way she put it he lost both his nerve and his hard on. Especially when she said, "Try to use it, I promise you'll lose it," as she cocked back both hammers of the twelve. Then as he had tried to run with his pants around his ankles, she fired the right barrel, a special load of rock salt and alum intended for serious troublemakers. "His lily white ass must have burned and puckered for a month," she laughed.

Zip knew at that moment this was his kind of woman!

Stormy walked into the small kitchen and wrapped her arms around him. Nuzzling his neck she whispered, "You're one in a million, Zip. One in a million!"

In his heart Zip wanted to tell her his true mission, but this was the wrong place, wrong time!

"Coffee, Bright Eyes?" Zip asked.

"Coffee and a line sounds good," she replied.

Zip dropped the better part of two grams in a small sealed baggie on the kitchen table and said, "A two incher for me, you keep the rest. I have to be in Pensacola before dark," he half lied. "I make a promise, I keep a promise," he said as he patted his left vest pocket. "But I will say this part three of my trip is cancelled until I get back!" he said smiling.

Stormy replied with a grin as she chopped up the meth, "I give everyone three strikes, Zip. If I haven't seen you in thirty days, Strike One. And you better have flowers in yur hand if you walk through that door one hour after thirty days!"

"I don't plan to be gone that long. But—!" and Zip left it at that.

Stormy gave Zip a passionate kiss as he walked out of the camper, and stood at the door as he fired up the Harley. She waved goodbye as he drove away. He smiled and blew a kiss with two fingers as he throttled up to the road leading the way.

Zip rode to Slidell, Louisiana, checked into a cheap hotel, showered, relaxed, charged up his cell phone and waited patiently.

*****

The Deal

At four am the next morning Zip's cell phone began to chime the tune "Charge of the Light Brigade." He had loved that tune ever since Nam.

"Zip speaking, your nickel," Zip mumbled.

"Hey, dude. This is Tater. You gave me your number, remember?"

"Yeah, man. I remember. At Sneaky's down by the river," Zip replied.

"Can you meet me somewhere, dude?"

"No problem. I'm on my way back from Pensacola."

"You know Log Town Landing?"

"Yeah, I'm familiar with it."

"Six pm. Bring your fishing pole and plenty of bait. You know what I'm talking about. Sit on the dock and I'll meet you there. Be alone!"

"Six pm. I'll be there. Later man." Zip hung up first.

Step two had just gone into motion. Zip took a quick shower, combed back his hair and roll tied it so it didn't look too long. No use drawing the eye of the local law.

Zip made a quick stop at one of his bank's branches and withdrew ten thousand dollars. There was a little bank hassle, but he told them he was going to a car auction.

A quick look through the local papers and he found just what he was looking for; an old pickup under a thousand dollars. Hell, it only needed to last a day or two.

Zip had the seller follow him to his storage building. He would have loaded the bike on the truck, but the truck had a camper topper. He dropped the owner off, went straight to the license tag office and made the old truck legal. Looking at his watch he had plenty of time before six pm, but he wanted at least an hour to double check the meeting spot.

Zip was hoping for quantity more that quality on the meth. Hell, he would probably dump most of it or call his friend to move it on down the line. This wasn't about dope. It was about justice, pure and simple.

Zip arrived at Log Town Landing around three thirty pm. Log Town was a historic place in south Mississippi. Early in the 1800's the exploration and timber industry started here. For almost one hundred years logs were floated down the Pearl River and cut into house timber. Right here where Zip sat. In the early 1960's, NASA bought all the land in a deal with Uncle Sam, and placed a rocket engine testing facility there, displacing thousands of people from their ancestral homes. A twenty mile diameter circle was drawn up as a Buffer Zone in case of a major rocket explosion.

Log Town residents were paid for their land and forced to move. Their homes were moved as well, burned down or torn down, and all that remains now are Cemeteries, abandoned porch steps of brick or concrete, and building foundations.

Zip sat on the small pier of the local boat launch, a fishing rod he bought at Wal Mart for ten dollars with a rock tied to the end of the line. It was about 5:50 pm when he heard the boat motor coming slowly down the river.

Zip checked both his guns. One under his shirt and one in his boot.

One man in a boat, fishing rods scattered about, a five gallon bucket sat between the boat seats. Zip sat patiently, moving his rock occasionally. The boat eased to the pier; it was Tater.

"Havin' any luck?" he asked.

"No, but I hope to," Zip replied.

"Where's you motorsickle?" Tater questioned.

"Back at the house. Thought it best to look like I belonged here." And he did. John Deere cap, camo pants and a blue jean shirt with the sleeves cut off.

"Grab your gear and take a boat ride with me," Tater barked.

Zip picked up his rod and reeled in his rock. Tater laughed at him through rotting teeth. "Watcha plannin' on catching wit' a rock?" he asked.

Zip, not breaking a smile, replied, "Rock lobster."

Tater laughed a chilling laugh as Zip picked up the tackle box with exactly four thousand cash in it, and stepped into the boat then shoved off from the pier. An ice chest sat between the seats of the sixteen foot aluminum skiff. Tater opened up the lid and pulled out two Budweisers, pitching one to Zip as he slowly motored up stream. The river split into two channels, the East and West Pearl. Tater took the Western channel and motored silently. Zip waited patiently for him to make the first move.

The river widened to about one hundred yards across and Tater stopped the boat and dropped the anchor. The water was smooth and deep, at least forty feet. When the boat caught and sat idly in the weak current Tater pitched his beer can over the side.

"Want another?" Tater asked.

"Naw, still sipping on this one," Zip replied.

"You drink too slow, man," Tater laughed. This here part of the river is called Yankee Scream Run. Paw told us legend has it that the Johnny Rebs chased a dozen or so Yankee soldiers through the swamp. They got to that point up yonder and ran out of land, so's they jumped in the river, and the Rebs, well they just picked 'em off one by one as they floated down the river. Like shooting fish in a barrel!" Tater laughed again.

Downing the second beer and tossing the can, he opened the cooler again. This time he came up with a long barrel 44 Magnum and pointed it at Zip's chest.

Zip never flinched. He expected this, the "are you a narc?" scenario.

"OK, Mr. Harley Man, you working for the feds, the local law or anybody?"

"Nope," Zip chopped. "Just working for me."

"You packing Motherfucker," Tater snapped.

"Yep," Zip replied. "I'd be an idiot not to."

"Lay 'em on the boat seat, dude."

Zip slowly lifted his shirt and laid his prized Army .45 on the seat. Slowly pulling up his pants leg, he pulled the .45/410 out of his boot.

"Gawd damn, dude! You don't fuckin' play, do you?" Tater laughed. "OK, man, jump in. If you's wired I'm shorting you out!"

Zip baulked at jumping into the cold deep river fully clothed, but figured it best to play along, so over the side he went. When he surfaced Tater laid down his gun and extended his hand to pull Zip back in the boat.

"Sorry about all that, dude. But these days we gotta be careful. Folks getting busted left and right."

Zip shook the cold water from his hair and slicked it back, shivering as Tater pulled up the anchor and started the motor. As they rounded the next bend Tater began to deal.

"OK, dude. How much you want?"

"How much you got and what's the bottom line price. I'm cold and don't feel much like dicking around over money."

"I got one fresh ounce broke down into eight balls, two hundred fifty an eight unless you want it all. You want it all, eighteen hundred for the ounce."

"That's all you got is one ounce? I was hoping for at least three!"

"Well, my kinda customer. Just hand on a second." Reaching into a small tackle box Tater retrieved a small hand radio. "Two Bit, come in. Let go of your dick and answer the radio." Tater smiled.

The voice came back, "I ain't playing with my dick, I'm right here doin' like you tole me!" Two Bit barked.

"Awright, dipshit. I'm pulling up to the sand bar. Bring down that other tackle box. Everything is cool."

Tater slowly motored the boat up to the small sand bar on the West bank of the river. Two Bit walked out of the brush at the top of the bar, fully camo'ed, a scoped .30-06 over his shoulder and a small tackle box in his hand.

"I like you boys," Zip remarked. "Real careful and you cover your ass!"

"Got to be careful. We're both third strikers. One more and it's life without parole!"

Tater sneered.

Two Bit walked to the boat and pulled it onto the sand bar. He sat the tackle box next to his brother and stood silently.

"Two more O.Z's," Tater said.

Zip picked up the tackle box and sat it on the boat seat. "Four large in the box, another wet two in my pocket. Bust me out a line and give me five minutes for a kick. If it's all good, we're good."

"Well, that's about four hundred dollars short ain't it, Harley Man? I may be from the swamp but I can still count," Tater snapped.

"I had to get wet, and that's all I brought. I really didn't expect you to have more than one or two ounces. Take it or leave it, it's all the same to me, man. It's all about the money," Zip lied.

Smiling, Tater opened one of the plastic pouches and cut out three fat lines of meth about four inches long. Once again Two Bit produced a straw and handed it to Zip. Zip took half a line up each nostril and immediately his eyes watered and his sinuses burned. In less that two minutes the speed rush hit.

"Good shit," was all Zip could say.

"Best in these here parts," Tater replied as he snorted his line, handing the straw back to Two Bit.

"Best fuckin' anhydrous in the South, straight from Hitler's recipe," laughed Two Bit. As he held his nose with one hand and wiped the tears from his eyes on his opposite shirt sleeve.

"All's good," said Tater. "We square on this one. Jus' let me know how much next time I call you. If'n you want more than four ounces I can drop the price to fifteen hundred per. But less that four is gonna be eighteen hundred. And I'll cut you slack for today since you been straight up!"

"Then we're square. Take me back to the pier," Zip said handing over the tackle box and wet roll of cash from his pocket.

Tater handed the tackle box and money roll to Two Bit, who then pushed the skiff back into the river. Half way back to the pier Tater told Zip to pick up his guns, shook his hand and said, "Nice doin' business with you."

Zip wanted to wash his hand instantly, but he had big plans in store for these two.

Over the next two weeks three more similar deals went down. Trust was established and a comfort level set.

On the fourth transaction, Zip invited the Vest brothers up to his place.

It was time for justice.

* * * * *

Justice

Zip had been a busy man over the last three days. The Vest brothers had taken him to their house boat on the last transaction. It was an old abandoned barge that had been left in the bayou back in the late '20's when the timber industry had finished raping the swamp, and the Great Depression hit. Even though it was still afloat, it couldn't be moved out. Cypress trees had filled the bayou and all but sealed off the small lake where it rested. Paw Paw Vest had somehow found it in the '50's, bought ten acres surrounding the lake and was just on the outskirt edge of the NASA

Buffer Zone. It was the perfect outlaw's hideaway. Like the famous pirate from the early 1800's Pierre Remeaux, the Vest brothers considered them-selves the King's of Honey Island. Only they had no honor or dignity. Their's was money, perversion, and reject power.

On his last transaction at the houseboat Zip had purchased five ounces, a total of seventy five hundred dollars. The Vest brothers were happy and Zip was burning. Now that trust had been established it was time for justice. Zip had watched every little thing that went on at the houseboat: Where the guns were, where the money went, where the dope was stashed, he watched it all. Another plan in motion.

Zip had called his boss to let him know all was well and he was back on the land. The Boss in turn said, Good job. Not to worry. All was quiet in New Orleans and that they may come out to the camp for Fourth of July. But nothing definite yet. To just keep up the good job, blah, blah, blah.

Zip had spent the night on one of the sand hills near the abandoned gravel pit. He said a prayer to the God, the Creator, and asked the Spirits to guide him in his mission. Zip was at peace with himself and with the justice that was forthcoming.

The day before the next transaction a glitch came into the plan. Zip had stopped at the local liquor store in Pear River Louisiana. There he saw the poster in the window.

MISSING
Suzzanne Comeaux
Age   17
5' 6"   135 pounds
Brown hair, brown eyes
Last seen at Slidell movie theater.
Possible runaway, possible abduction.
Blah, blah, blah
St. Tammany Police Department

Zip began to burn. Now there was more than the Vest brothers to deal with, but they may have kidnapped another young girl. He remembered the other child had been missing for over three weeks, so they like to play with them a while. With luck he could save this one before too much damage was done. But any damage was too much. His rage flared but he could not let it cloud his judgment.

Zip had everything he needed for his plan. With this new twist he would have to alter a few things, but he could still make it work. A phone cal to one of his boss's associates, a prominent doctor in New Orleans, took care of what he needed.

The Doc couldn't argue. Zip had never asked for anything and had cleaned up after the Doc on three separate occasions. Doc had a passion for cocaine and young transvestites. Zip got what he needed with no questions asked.

The cell phone chimed and Zip answered on the third chime. "Zip here. Your nickel."

"It's Tater, Harley Man. Be there in five or less. Just crossing the bridge on the interstate!" Tater said.

"I'll be at the gate to let you in, man. Drive careful. Lots of H.P. out today." Zip was beaming.

All of the preparations had been made, an elaborate truth extracting area by the abandoned gravel pits. A fresh fifth of Jack Daniels, a fresh fifth of Southern Comfort laced with enough "roofies" to put them out for at least six hours, the seals carefully steamed loose and reglued to look unbroken.

A small tape recorder for the confessions and three hungry twelve foot babies in the old abandoned pit. The plan was about to come together.

The old model Chevy Blazer pulled up to the gate, and Zip stepped out of the brush to unlock it. The Vest brothers pulled through and zip relocked the gate. Jumping on to the hood of the old four wheel drive he pointed to the right. About another hundred yards they were at Zip's little cabin on the river.

"Hey, man, I know this place. I been fishing up here for years," Two Bit babbled. "Thought some rich dick in New Orleans owned it."

"One does, I'm just the care taker. The big camp is way in the back. He only comes once or twice a year to hunt deer. Rest of the time it's just me and the animals," Zip explained.

"Pretty damn secluded set up, Harley Man. Kinda like us, quiet, private, out of the way but close to what you need. Bet you have you some good fun out here with the Honeys, dontcha?" Tater laughed.

"Fun is fun and business is business, and this is strictly business," Zip replied.

"Let's go have a drink, a line and take care of business."

"This stuff as good as the last?" Zip asked.

"Probably better. This here is something new, a new recipe somebody turned us on to. It's called "glass". Takes less, lasts longer and one hell of a high," Tater beamed.

This bothered Zip a little. He had done "glass" before and he didn't want to lose focus or control.

"Bust it up and let's give it a try," Zip laughed, stepping behind his bar.

Tater and Two Bit took a seat on the bar stools as Tater opened the small tackle box he was carrying. Zip sat an eight by eight mirror on the bar and chose a package from the box. Tater did the lines out and once again Two Bit provided the straw. They each did a line and Zip felt the effects almost immediately.

"Gentlemen, this is some good shit. What's it gonna cost me?" Zip asked.

"Ten large, Harley Man. But you'll triple your money back at two hundred a gram," Tater exclaimed.

"Sounds good. Let's drink to that," Zip replied. "Two Bit, you're a Southern Comfort man, right? And Tater Jack Black, correct?"

"You got a good memory, Harley Man," Tater exclaimed.

Zip sat the two sealed bottles on the bar and a bucket of ice.

"You boys straight up men, or you need a chaser?" Zip asked.

"Straight for me, no ice," said Two Bit.

"Bud back, if I can get one," said Tater.

Zip sat a Bud from the small refrigerator on the bar and turned his back to the painting of Crazy Horse on the wall.

"Just give me a second and I'll cover your money," Zip said.

Swinging the painting back and revealing a hidden wall safe, Zip made a few turns on the combination knob and opened it up. Counting out ten stacks he turned back to see Tater and Two Bit wide eyed and staring.

Zip spread the stacks across the bar and said, "What's wrong, boys? Drink up. I know to be prepared this time!"

"It's just that you ain't drinking and it's hard to trust a man who ain't drinking with me," Tater quipped.

"My bad, Tater. When I'm at home I'm a scotch man!" Zip said as he pulled a bottle of single malt from the shelf beneath the bar. The bottled had been prepared with something from the Doc to counter the effects of the speed and keep Zip together.

Zip dropped two cubes of ice in a glass and poured a generous helping. Raising his glass in a toast Zip said "Here's to good dope, good profit, and good pussy!"

"I'll drink to that," said Tater.

"Me, too," answered Two Bit. After only three drinks Two Bit was on the floor and Tater wasn't far behind. Zip was straight, focused and pumped for what was to come.

* * * * *

Justice!

It was a little trouble getting the two limp bodies of the Vest brothers down the stairs and into the littler trailer attached to the four wheel drive ATV, but nothing Zip couldn't handle. Zip hummed a little tune to himself as he drove his cargo to the back of the abandoned gravel pit.

It took less than an hour to get them properly tied up and in position for their trial and judgment. Hooking up the IV's had been the hardest part, but Zip had done his homework, and his patients felt absolutely nothing at this moment.

Zip had fashioned the racks from good strong timber, the ropes and pulleys were quite elaborate. Both the Vest brothers had been stripped naked and hung spread eagle on the racks, facing each other at a distance of about four feet. A small generator quietly hummed in the distance. The bright lights were just waiting to be turned on. A small lantern on a table cast a low glow.

Zip had become quite an electronics wizard in the past few years, learning much from his young friends about computers and sound and audio systems. The micro speakers had been placed to achieve maximum effect. The microphones to record just what Zip wanted. Information and confessions.

Zip had changed clothes, now wearing black leather pants and an executioner's hood mainly just for shock value. Underneath the hood a headset microphone, wireless direct to the sound system, and a voice distortion device that made Zip sound like a demon from someone's worst nightmare.

Zip injected the drugs to bring them around into the IV tubes and stood back in the glow of the lantern and waited. Surprisingly Two Bit was the first to recover. Having been out on the "roofies" and whiskey for about four hours the detox shot brought him to reality rather quickly.

Suspended about a foot from the ground spread eagle and naked on a rack can be a rather sobering experience in its self.

Once his vision had cleared and his head lifted he began to scream.

"What the fuck? Where the hell? Tater! Tater, man, what the fuck!"

He was quickly silenced with the ball gag that Zip had purchased in New Orleans.

Caught from behind in the dim light of the lantern, Two Bit didn't see Zip as the executioner. When Tater began to come around a few minutes later Two Bit saw the executioner as he gagged Tater with a similar leather and ball gag. Two Bit fainted and had to be given another hit to bring him back.

Zip wanted both men up. He wanted them to feel their pain. He wanted justice that no court could ever give.

Zip hit the button on the remote. It brought up the bright lights, the music from Dante's Inferno and turned on the video cameras and tape recorders.

"Sinners, welcome to Hell!" This distortion enhanced the voice of Zip. "I'll ask the questions. The correct answers will give you life. Incorrect answers will bring you pain and eventually Death. Who will speak first? Just nod and wiggle around if you please."

Both men began to shake, attempt to scream, or speak. Zip just let them vent their rage until they settled down. Zip had already figured Two Bit for the weakest. So he would work on Tater first. Dimming the lights he removed Tater's gag.

"Mother fucker, you a dead man, I get out of this shit! You a dead man!" Tater lashed out. "Who the fuck are you? Where the hell is Harley Man? Why you fucking with us?"

"Harley Man has already gone to his reward," Zip spoke casually.

"As for you two, you have questions to answer. Once again, right answers will gain your freedom, wrong ones will gain you pain."

Bringing the lights and music up again, this time the music was Native American drum and chant. Zip let it play for about five minutes as Tater struggled and cursed. Two Bit hung silently with tears running down his cheeks.

Zip brought the music down and rolled a medical cart within sight of both men. Slowly he uncovered the top tray, an assortment of scalpels, bone saws, knives and other instruments in clear view. Two Bit could only quiver and moan. Tater cursed, "Bring it on, motherfucker! You ain't from shit!"

Zip asked his first question.

"Tell me about Mellissa Baxter?"

"Fuck you, asshole! I don't know no Mellissa fucking Baxter!" Tater spit.

"Wrong answer," Zip said picking up the surgeons scalpel and stepping behind Tater. Zip made a small cut about a half inch wide the distance from shoulder to hip, and then a second cut from the opposite side of the half inch width. Zip had done a lot a homework since the death of Mellissa Baxter.

The Chinese had preferred this torture a thousand years ago, the "Death of a Thousand Cuts." In essence skinning a human being one small strip at a time. Tater began to scream in agony. Two Bit tried to scream but could only moan through the ball gag. Zip finished the first 'peel' and Tater passed out.

Zip let him hang and walked up to Two Bit. In his distorted voice Zip asked, "If I remove your gag and ask you the same question I asked him, will I receive a correct answer?"

Two Bit nodded hysterically yes. Regagging the unconscious Tater, Zip released Two Bit's gag and softly asked, "Tell me about Mellissa Baxter?"

Two Bit began to ramble. "She was a little prissy bitch that always had something smart to say when me and Tater went to the movies up in Picayune. She was there every Friday night. If we went she'd say "There come those ol' stinky swamp men" or "something around here smells like a crawfish boil", and we ain't never said nothin' to that kid. An' the last time we was up there at the movies we'd cleaned up real good. Didn't smell bad or nothin' and she said sumthin' I didn't hear. But it set Tater off real bad. In the middle of the movie Tater said he was going to pee and he was gone about fifteen minutes. When he came back he was all smiles. I figured he'd gone out to the Blazer and done a line or two. We left the movie and started back to the swamp when I heard something moving around in the back of the Blazer. Tater had done hit her with that leather rag an' put her in the Blazer all tied up. I started to say something an' Tater tole me to shush up, that we had something' to play with for a while, and that the little bitch had a lesson coming. So we took her back to the swamp and played with her a while, just like paw taught us, and when Tater said it was getting' old we fed her to the gators just like Paw taught us. Man I tole you the truth; just don't hurt me no more!"

Zip felt his rage soar trying to keep control. He had his confession but not his justice. Zip picked up a stun gun from the table top and put it to Two Bit's neck. "Good night," Zip said and hit the button. Two Bit jerked and quivered then went limp. Fifty thousand volts packs quite a punch.

Zip replaced Two Bit's gag and returned to Tater. The second the wake up drug hit Tater's vein he came to cursing and screaming. Zip let him vent his rage until he settled down.

"Now I already learned from your brother about Mellissa Baxter. Tell me about the ones before?" Zip asked, changing the distortion voice and turning the strobe light on, dimming the bright lights and once again changing the music to heavy metal. Three more skin strips, two fingers and two toes later Zip had almost everything he wanted from Tater. Tater was listless but still very much alive and in much pain. Zip had used a butane torch to cauterize the fingers and toes. The skin strips wouldn't bleed for long. Hell the Chinese kept men alive for days with the same torture.

Two Bit had come around on his own and moaned, groaned and fought against his bonds the entire time he was being questioned. Time had passed and the moon was up and nearly full. Zip regagged Tater and let him hang. Returning to Two Bit he removed his gag.

"One final question," Zip asked, turning off the strobe, bringing the bright lights back up and once again changing the music. This time something soft and soothing, elevator music Zip had called it before making this special CD.

"Anything, man, just don't hurt me or Tater no more, man. Please!" he whined.

"Suzzanne Comeaux from Slidell?"

Two Bit began to cry and beg. "Man, she's in the Hidey Hole under the kitchen in the houseboat, man. We just took her, man, we ain't even done her yet, man. We just started training her, like Paw taught us. She's gonna be tough 'cause she's older. I wanted one with some titties, man. I wanted a woman not a little girl. Paw and Tater always wanted them young ones . . ."

Zip could not hold back any longer. Picking up the stun gun from the table he put Two Bit's lights out, regretting what he had done, letting rage take over. Zip sat for a few moments and cried. First tears in ages. "May God have mercy on me for what I'm about to do, but there must be justice!" Zip cried again to the sky.

Zip had more than confessions on tape, he had the knowledge that another young girl was locked up in a dark damp hole in the swamp and no one else but him and the rejects knew about her. One more life dangling like a puppet on a string.

Zip laid himself out a line of crystal, poured himself a shot of scotch and finished what he started.

Zip pulled the strange contraption he had rigged up between the two hanging men, ran the strings and wires, placed all the pulleys and locked on the nuts and bolts. He placed the two twelve gauge shotguns in their racks, loaded, cocked and ready. Slipping on a pair of surgical gloves, Zip tied a string, just behind the head of each man's penis. An elaborate set up, but a genuine means to an end. Each gun was pointed at the opposite brother. Which ever one reached an erection first would blow the brains out of the other, and the video tape still rolled.

Zip hit the IV again with the wake up drug. Both men rallied, cursing and screaming until Zip gagged each yet again. Zip then rolled a T.V. where both men could see, then he spoke as he prepared two syringes, a different distortion voice again. "Brothers, I have all I want from you now. Now one of you must choose who lives and who dies. It may be one, it may be both. It may be neither. It is your choice!" Stepping out of the video camera range Zip hit the remote button. The TV came on, a three hour porno movie featuring young girls. Zip then injected them with something the Doc had called liquid Viagra, guaranteed to produce a raging hard on in thirty minutes or less, depending on the individual. Zip turned and walked into the darkness with the bottle of scotch.

Less than fifteen minutes had passed when the blast of a twelve gauge split the night silence. Zip slowly walked back. What was left of Tater hung limply in the rack. The pitiful sight of a sobbing Two Bit stretched out, moaning gagged and erect staring at his now almost headless brother. Zip began to move all the equipment, first cutting the string to Two Bit's still erect penis. Pulling out the video tape he secured it in a case and stashed it on the ATV. Zip took his time loading up all the equipment. Now for the final clean up.

Less than an hour had passed, the sun was beginning to rise over the swamp. A morning mist of fog spread from the river and the bayous. The body of what was once Wilmer "Tater" Vest lay on the sand. Two Bit, now wide eyed having been given a booster shot of crystal meth, still hung helpless in the rack, nothing else around except the IV bottle and a blood trail of chicken entrails leading down to an abandoned gravel pit.

Two Bit turned his head to the small noise to his right just in time to see a figure turning on a video camera then fade back into the brush.

A grunting noise caught his attention, and he looked back at his dead brother. Some fifty feet away three large dark forms were working their way across the sand and toward him. It didn't take long for Two Bit to recognize a large gator, much less three of them. It did not take long for the gators to take Tater apart and carry him off to their dens. Two Bit hung helpless, too high to pass out, to scared to think. His brain was in overdrive, as well as his heart. Then a warm feeling came over him then darkness.

Zip pulled the next to the last syringe out of the IV tube, cut Two Bit down and dropped him in the trailer of the ATV. The liquid Demerol would keep him out for hours, enough time to load up and run down river.

Zip sacked up Two Bit and dropped him in the bottom of the small boat, covered him with nets and fishing equipment. Zip looked just like another working man out for a day of fishing. It took about an hour to reach the Vest brother's hideaway by boat.

Zip eased the boat up to the small pier by the houseboat. He drug Two Bit out of the boat and up the pier to the bank. Tying him securely to a small cypress tree Zip began his search for the other missing girl.

It didn't take long for Zip to find her. Beneath the rug that the kitchen table sat on was a trap door. A set of stairs led into the bowels of the old barge. A well constructed sound proof room. On the walls were dozens of Polaroid photos of young girls. The photos were dated, some were just of the girls, some where they were obviously being forced into sex acts with the brothers. Some with a man who must have been Paw Paw Vest. A wave of nausea came over Zip when he saw the pleading eyes of the young child Mellissa Baxter. Her battered face, her lost stare, the same eyes that started him on this mission several weeks ago.

Zip swayed in a dizzy, sick wave of anger and pain. His entire life flashed before him. His youth, Viet Nam, the years of wandering, his fast few years as caretaker and clean up man. All the bad, now one chance of making amends with himself and the creator. Zip located a bolted, pad locked door in the corner of the room. A set of keys hung from a nail on the door frame. Zip tried all the keys until one opened the lock. He stepped into the room. His hand bumped something in the darkness, a single light bulb suspended on a cord. Zip turned on the light and adjusted his vision. Drawn up in the corner of the room on an old stained mattress was Suzzanne Comeaux, naked and shackled at her ankle. A gallon bottle of water, a few pieces of moldy bread and a five gallon bucket for relieving herself, were all that were in the room.

Covering her eyes at the brightness of the light she pleaded, "Don't hurt me any more. I'll do what you want. Just don't leave me in the dark with the rats and the roaches. I'll do everything you wanted! Please just let me out!"

"Suzzanne Comeaux?" Zip asked.

"Yesss," she cried weakly.

"I'm here to help you. Just calm down, My name's Bubba and I ain't gonna hurt you, OK?" Zip lied about his name, but not about his intentions. Stepping back into the other room he found a blanket, a pair of blue jeans that could be hers and a t shirt and jacket. All were dirty and tattered but at least she could cover herself.

Returning to the room Zip laid the clothes and blanket on the mattress. She grabbed the blanket and covered herself. Zip began turning keys to unlock the shackle. Finally the right one popped the lock. She drew her feet up under the blanket and stared at Zip.

Trying to keep his face away from her he was trying to come up with a quick plan to get her safely home and finish what he had to do.

"I'm gonna step out here so you can get some clothes on, then we're gonna get outta here!" Zip drawled, trying hard to fake a good ol' boy accent.

"Okay, " was all she could say.

Walking out of the room, still skittish, wondering if 'Bubba' Zip was one of her captors or someone really here to help. Zip led the climb out of the room and into the kitchen. She followed slowly, still in fear. She followed Zip out into the sunlight, first time in three days. The sun hurt her eyes but she followed on.

As they started down the pier to the boat she spotted the unconscious Two Bit tied to the cypress tree, naked and flat on his ass on the ground, head rolling in Demerol euphoria. Flinging off the blanket and flying into a rage she charged him.

"You motherfucker! You bastard! You filthy son of a bitch!" she screamed, swinging fists and feet. 'Bubba' Zip let her vent hate and rage. Pulling her back Zip softly spoke. "Come on, girl. Let's get you home." Zip pulled her back to the pier and into the boat. She sat silently staring at Two Bit on the bank.

Zip 'Bubba' cranked the motor under the boat, and motored slowly out of the swamp back to the main river. Suzanne sat silently looking at him. When they reached the main river Zip killed the motor and let the boat drift with the current downstream.

"Who are you really, and how did you know my name?" Suzanne asked.

"Your picture is on every window from New Orleans to the Gulf Coast, and as far north as Hattiesburg, Mississippi," Zip said quietly.

"What about you, dude? You don't have fisherman's hands, they're too soft," she said looking him directly in the eyes.

As Zip held her eyes he could sense that she may be young, but she was smart. She was no innocent to the world, like the Vest brothers' other victims. "If I share something with you, can you keep it totally to yourself?" Zip asked softly.

"I've been in trouble since I was fourteen and I've never ratted out nobody," she said, dropping her head. "But I thought this was my last rodeo," she added.

Biographical Notes

Wendy Babiak is the author of *Conspiracy of Leaves* (Plain View Press). Her poems have appeared in/at *Tampa Review, Barrelhouse, Free Inquiry, No Tell Motel, Big Bridge,* and *Poems Against War*, among others. She and her family have settled in Ithaca, NY, recently, after a lifetime of hassle for being a hippy (i.e., caring). She can be found discussing her engaged poetics, and all that it engages, at http://wbabiak.wordpress.com.

Lee Balan, after a career in mental health, returned to writing and art. He was the first editor and art director for Beyond Baroque Magazine in Venice, CA. He has had poems and stories featured in several magazines including *Phantom Seed, Sun Runner,* and *Storylandia.* He was the facilitator for the Tenderloin Writer's Workshop in San Francisco. His background in mental health has been a major influence on his work. Lee Balan's first novel *Alien Journal* has recently been published by Blood Soup Books in Palm Springs, CA.

Jill Battson is an internationally published poet and poetry activist who is currently the Poet Laureate of Cobourg, Ontario. She was responsible for creating and running the successful poetry reading series The Poets' Refuge and has initiated and produced many poetry events including The Poetry Express—a BYOV at Toronto's Fringe Festival; Liminal Sisters—a language poetry event; The Festival of the Spoken Word—a five day spoken word festival; Fightin' Words—poets in a boxing ring; The Poetburo Slams and the hyper successful Word Up—a series of interstitial poetry spots airing on MuchMusic and Bravo! which spawned a CD with Virgin Records and an anthology with Key Porter. She was the poetry editor for Insomniac Press from 1999 to 2001. Jill is widely published across North America and in the UK. Her first book, *Hard Candy*, received great acclaim and was nominated for the Gerald Lampert Award. She has written several plays and solo works, including *How I Learned to Live With Obsession*, as well as *Ecce Homo* and *Hard Candy*—enhanced monologues for dance and voice. She has written the libretti for two short operas, Netsuke and Ashlike on the Cradle of the Wind, produced by Tapestry New Opera Works, and produced an electro acoustic sound art project, LinguaElastic, as part of the Canadian Music Centre's New Music in New Places series. Dark Star Requiem, for which she wrote the libretto, premiered at Toronto's Luminato Festival in June 2010. Jill's third book of poems, *Dark Star Requiem*, was recently published by Folded & Gathered Press. <jillspoetbureau.blogspot.com >

Dianne Borsenik, a former flowerchild and current redhead, is active in the Cleveland, Ohio, poetry scene. Her work has appeared in a diverse number of places and publications, including *Slipstream*, *The Magnetic Poetry Book of Poetry*, the Cleveland RTA 2008 and 2009 Poetry Projects, the Wick Poetry Center's Peace Speaks art project, the Crisis Chronicles Online Library, the 2010 Poetry Bomb tour, and in actor Jonathan Frid's show Genesis of Evil. With poetry partner John Burroughs, she coproduces and cohosts the monthly Lix & Kix Poetry Extravaganza at Bela Dubby's Art Gallery and Beer Cafe.

Cynthia Bryant. In the spring of 1967, Cynthia Bryant ran away from a troubled home to San Francisco in search of a better life. Her poetry reflects a unique life journey and the relentless continuation of that search. Cynthia was the Poet Laureate of Pleasanton, CA from 2005–2007 and maintains the website www.poetslane.com

John Burroughs, a.k.a. Jesus Crisis, is a poet and musician based in Elyria, Ohio. He founded the Crisis Chronicles Online Library and co hosts the monthly Lix and Kix Poetry Extravaganza. Find him at www.crisischronicles.com

Donald R. Carson, Sr., a Navy veteran, poet and a country boy from West Virginia, now makes his home in North Carolina. After spending years in Cleveland, Ohio, he made his way back to his country roots where he continues to write poetry and talk to nature. He is the father of author and poet Diana May-Waldman who says, "My father was a poet, first and foremost. But, life got in the way. He was raising children during the 60s, was on the picket lines and fighting for the union. Scotch on ice and a manual typewriter. He always said, 'Never write a Dear John letter and never treat anyone with disrespect in your own home, because you have the advantage and it's no longer fair.' My father gave me a million words. Thanks Dad."

Michael Castro is a poet living in St. Louis, where in 1975 he co founded the literary organization River Styx, which produces *River Styx Magazine* and the River Styx at Duff's Poetry Series. He hosted the poetry radio program Poetry Beat 1989 2003. His most recent poetry productions are the books *The Bush Years* (JK Publishing 2010), and *A Transparent Lion: Selected Poems of Attila Jozsef* (Green Integer Books, 2006), co-translated from the Hungarian with Gabor G. Gyukics; and the CD, Kokopilau, with saxophonist J.D. Parran (Freedonia Music 2009).

Jim Christy is a widely published writer and a visual artist who has exhibited throughout the world. Raised in Philadelphia, he left the United States due to political differences. He lives on a farm in Ontario when not traveling. As a reporter he covered seven wars and has been out in the field on mine clearing crews in Cambodia. He frequently reads his poetry with jazz or blues groups.

Susan Deer Cloud is a Catskill Native of Mohawk / Seneca / Blackfoot lineage. She has received various awards and fellowships, including a National Endowment for the Arts Literature Fellowship, a New York State Foundation for the Arts Fellowship, a Chenango County Council for the Arts Literature Grant, First Prize in Allen Ginsberg Poetry Competition (twice), Prairie Schooner's Readers' Choice Award, and Native American Wordcraft Circle Editor's Award for her multicultural anthology Confluence. Most recently her poems "Car Stealer" and "Ode to O Holy Nights in Liberty, NY" were finalist and semi-finalist in Many Mountains Moving Poetry Competition ("Car Stealer" is in Spring 2010 MMM issue). Deer Cloud's poems and stories have been published in numerous journals and anthologies (*Sister Nations: an Anthology of Native Women Writers on Community*, *Unsettling America* & *Identity Lessons* multicultural anthologies, *American Indian Culture & Research Journal*, *Yellow Medicine Review*, *To Topos* (Poetry International), *Florida Review*, *Mid-American Review*, *Ms. Magazine*, *Prairie Schooner*, *Many Mountains Moving*, *North Dakota Quarterly*, *Quarterly West*, *Earth's Daughters*, *Shenandoah*, *Blood Lotus*, *Exquisite Corpse*, *Pembroke Magazine*, *Stone Canoe*, *Paterson Literary Review*, *Helicon Nine*, etc.).

Geri Digiorno. Sonoma county Poet Laureate (2006 2007) and artist, Geri Digiorno is founder and director of the Petaluma Poetry Walk, an annual literary event celebrating its 15th anniversary. Her most recent book of poems is *Rosetta Mary* (dPress,2007) and *White Lipstick* (Red Hen Press, 2005).

DubbleX is a poet, writer and musician, and graffiti artist who spends his days being certifiably crazy. DubbleX has been writing & playing music his entire life. He has been published by *Street Literature Review Magazine* (paper) *The Cartier Street Review*, *the Nov. 3 rd Club*, *Polarity*, *Mad Swirl*, *readerjack.com*, *wheelhouse magazine*, and the recent *Omega 7*. DubbleX writes & plays music to stay sane.

Gloria Frym is the author of two collections of short stories—*Distance No Object* (City Lights Books), and *How I Learned* (Coffee House Press) Her most recent books of poetry are *The Lost Sappho Poems* (Effing Press) and

Solution Simulacra (United Artists Books, 2006). A previous collection, *Homeless at Home* (Creative Arts Book Company), won an American Book Award in 2002. In 2010, Effing Press will bring out a new book of poems, *Mind Over Matter*. She teaches at California College of the Arts in the Bay Area.

Timothy Gager is the author of eight books of short fiction and poetry. His latest, *Treating a Sick Animal: Flash and Micro Fictions* (Cervena Barva Press) features over forty stories, many previously published in various literary magazines. He hosts the Dire Literary Series in Cambridge, Massachusetts every month and is the co-founder of Somerville News Writers Festival.
http://www.timothygager.com, http://www.whlreview.com, and http://www.somervillenewswritersfestival.com

William H.. Harrison, Jr. (Bill) a.k.a. Medicine Bill—world traveler, now at home in small town of his birth, Cockrum. MS. Musician poet, songwriter. "Last of my breed! Continually trying to make sense out of madness! Living, learning, loving on a daily basis—the love of life creed!"

Laura Strathman Hulka is a writer, reader, researcher, photographer, and crafter. She is a lifelong Californian, with brief nine-year span living in Tennessee, learning to speak Southern. She and her husband Ed retired to Rio Vista in 2009, choosing to live in a quaint, older mobile home so they could be close to the river. Laura is an ardent reader, writer, professional book reviewer and editor. She also works as a researcher and newsletter editor. She is the mother of two and the grandmother of two. She loves to explore the Delta byways, and is a firm believer in "blue highways," those small rambling roads that often lead to the best discoveries!

James Lee Jobe has been published in *Manzanita, Tule Review, Pearl*, and many other periodicals. His poems are also included in *The Sacramento Anthology: One Hundred Poems*; *Jewel Of The Valley: A California Anthology*; and *How To Be This Man: The Walter Pavlich Memorial Anthology*. From 1994 to 1999 Jobe was the editor and publisher of One Dog Press, a poetry monthly. He also edited the quarterly *Clan Of The Dog*. Jobe has 4 chapbooks published, the most recent is *What God Said When She Finally Answered*, Rattlesnake Press. His poetry blog is at jamesleejobe.wordpress.com.

Paul Krassner's autobiography is entitled, *Confessions of a Raving, Unconfined Nut: Misadventures in the Counterculture*. A new expanded edition is now available at paulkrassner.com

Angel Lambert grew up in Wellington, Ohio. She has been writing poetry since she was a child. She decided to scratch that itch during her junior year in high school. "There is not much time for writing nowadays, with a husband, four sons, and an ever growing pile of unfinished quilting projects, but peace is so important. Peace is not simply being still to rest or lack of conflict; it's a mindset. To live peaceably, one must learn to respect and enjoy others!"

Joy Leftow calls writing her first love. Her honesty and openness will floor you, maybe embarrass you but she promises not to bore you. Editor of *The Cartier Street Review* and double alumna from Columbia University with a second Masters from CCNY in Creative Writing, Leftow has been featured on Rockland Internet Radio, Indie Feed, Jazz Poetry Café, and Everything Goes. Her publications are too numerous to list here. Leftow has been called poet laureate of Washington Heights, the New York City neighborhood from which she hails. Leftow has won several poetry awards from various online college sites. Her book, *A Spot of Bleach and Other Poems & Prose* was published by Big Foot Press in 2006 and is available at Amazon.com and she is published in numerous other online and paper journals. Her work can be relished at http://joyleftowsblog.blogspot.com.

Skye Leslie is a poet and writer who attempts, daily, to live at the intersection of grace and reconciliation. Published in several online ezines, she is currently at work completing a book of poems and a book of creative non fiction. Her influences are primarily from American literary poets and fiction writers and as a survivor of domestic violence, has a passion for the stories of women from all walks of life.

Stephen Lewandowski has published ten small books of poetry. His poems and essays have appeared in regional and national environmental and literary journals and anthologies. He is a graduate of Hamilton College. He did graduate work with Louis Jones in the Cooperstown Graduate Programs in American Folk Culture and with Howard Nemerov and William Gass at Washington University in St. Louis. Lewandowski has worked as an environmental educator and consultant in the western Finger Lakes for thirty years. He is a founder of the Coalition for Hemlock and Canadice Lakes and the Canandaigua Lake Watershed Task Force. He is currently employed as the Program Director of the Lake Ontario Coastal Initiative. He has received the environmental achievement awards from the

Finger Lakes Community College, Canandaigua Lake Pure Waters, and the Finger Lakes Land Trust. He was elected to the Naples Town and Village Boards and has served on boards and advisory committees to the Finger Lakes Land Trust, Ganondagan State Historic Site, Rochester Committee for Scientific Information, NYS Open Space Committee, and the Cornell College of Agriculture and Life Sciences. He has been acknowledged as a Graduate of Distinction of Canandaigua Academy for his work in the arts and the environment and currently serves on the Board of Pegasus Early Music and the 1816 Farmington Quaker Meetinghouse Museum. His chapbook of poems, *O Lucky One* was published by Foothills Publishing of Kanona, NY in 2010. His work is forthcoming or has recently been published in *Bellowing Ark, The Scream, Hanging Loose, Free Verse, The Kerf, Puella Mea, House Organ, Stone Canoe* and *Blueline*. His essays have been published electronically at www.Rochesterblog.com, www,crookedlakereview.com, and www.yorkstaters.blogspot.com .

Lyn Lifshin. Recent books from Lifshin include: *The Licorice Daughter: My Year With Ruffian* (Texas Review Press), *Another Woman Who Looks Like Me* (Black Sparrow at Godine), following *Cold Comfort and Before It's Light, Desire and 92 Rapple*. She has over 120 books & has edited 4 anthologies. Also out recently: *Nutley Pond, Persephone, Barbaro: Beyond Brokenness, Lost In The Fog, Light At The End, Jesus Poems* and *Ballet Madonnas, Katrina, Lost Horses and Chiffon*. And coming soon: *All The Poets Who Have Touched Me, Living and Dead. All True: Especially The Lies And Ballroom*. Her website is www.lynlifshin.com

Teck Loh is an unfulfilled dreamer and previously unpublished writer from Singapore. He first achieved consciousness as a person when he visited London in 1999. That was his first visit to the West. His further education in Humanism continued when he, in a break from tradition and cliche, traveled to California from the Far East seeking instruction in the martial arts. There he encountered NRA members and hippies who taught him all he now knows about Freedom. He currently resides in Singapore.

David Meltzer was raised in Brooklyn during the War years and performed on radio & early TV on the Horn & Hardart Childrenos Hour. Exiled to L.A. at 16, he enrolled in an ongoing academy w/ artists Wallace Berman, George Herms, Robert Alexander, Cameron; then migrated to San Francisco in l957 for higher education with Jack Spicer, Robert Duncan, Joanne Kyger, Diane DiPrima, Michael McClure, Lew Welch, Philip Whalen, Jack Hirschman, and many more. In 2005, *Beat Thing* (La Alameda Press, 2004) won the Josephine Miles PEN Award, and *David's*

Copy: The Selected Poems of David Meltzer which spans over forty years of work, was published by Viking/Penguin.

Martha Meltzer. http://www.myspace.com/marthameltzer "I always thought you'd grow up to be a poet," he said, cigarette smoke curling around the words.

Michelle Close Mills is a closet hippie masquerading as a middle aged mom. Her poetry and short stories have appeared in many short story anthologies including *Chicken Soup for the Recovering Soul—Daily Inspirations, Chicken Soup for the Soul in Menopause, Chicken Soup for the Soul—A Mother's Devotional, To Have and To Hold: Prayers, Poems, and Blessings for Newlyweds*, as well as *The Ultimate Gardener* and *The Ultimate Bird Love* by HCI books. She has also written a poetry collection entitled Prisms in a *Looking Glass* available at Amazon.com. Michelle resides in Largo, Florida with her very cool husband, Ralph.

Jesse Mitchell is writer. He lives close to the soil in the wilds of rural southern Illinois with his wife and many children. His life is filled with books, craziness and love. See these links: www.findingthebeatmovie.com & www.open.salon.com/blog/jmitch79

Ars Moriendi – "Peace slipped under my door after years of living in violence. When it found me it was all that mattered. Love can shatter the most broken of hearts."

Craig Murray lives in Canada, where his time is divided between writing fiction, prose and poetry, and working with several volunteer organizations. Previously a decorated Army Captain he is now the Architectural Designer for a conservation authority. He has written four novels and is working on his fifth. He received a Pushcart nomination in 2004, a Best of the Net nomination in 2006 and his poetry and short fiction have been published in a number of print and online journals. His most recent publications include the the poetry book, *Watching Her Walk*, and the short story collection, *Atomic Memories*.

William Page's poetry and short fiction is in a number of "small" literary magazines in the U.S. His translation of *Les Diablogues* by Ronald Dubillard was published by the French Culture Services and performed in Los Angeles at the Tiffany Theater. It was the theater "pick of the week" in the LA Weekly, and the translation went on to be nominated for an Ovation award. The play The Heracles Chronicles will be performed this year at L'Espace Culturel de Mennecy in Paris in an English/French version. Pages's poetry can be found on his website: http://tiltyourhead.wordpress.com/

Seelan Palay is an artist and activist from Singapore. He works with Free Burma Campaign Singapore and blogs here http://seelanpalay.blogspot.com

Sherry Pasquarello is a Pittsburgh born and bred poet. She was the past administrator for the international PK LIST. Pasquarello is ad proud member of the Pittsburgh Woman's Blogging Society. Her work has been included in the The Anthology Project 2004, *The Writer's Hood, Four Volts U.K., Alchemy Lit. Mag, Caught in the Net*, WorldWide Hippies and numerous other journals. Pasquarello has been writing since the mid sixties. A mother and a grandmother, she also creates artisan cement garden stones and is passing on the love and ideals of hippiedom to her family.

Andrew J Pensabene III. currently resides in Ocean City, NJ. He practices chant and slowly learns the didgeridoo for trance and touching ones inner singularity! Poetry for him is a kind of personal science by which huge compressions of data and feeling further unfold deeper meaning and greater comprehension. Pensabene says, "Poems comprise a flow between our cranial hemispheres and hence through the temporal existence of flesh as a mad expression from deep within its history to the very distinct song of DNA."

Hans Plomp was born in Amsterdam in 1944. After his studies he became a teacher, but he gave up regular jobs for good when his first novel *De Ondertrouw* (The Banns Are Up) was successful. He took an active part in the playful Dutch Provo Revolution of the Sixties, which made Amsterdam one of the hippest places on the planet. After Provo, he helped found Culturele Vrijhaven Ruigoord, the Amsterdam Balloon Company, and the Fiery Tongues Poetry Festival, and he traveled extensively, especially in India, where he spent some five years. In 1982, he toured the U.S. with a group of prominent Dutch poets, performing with Anne Waldman, Diane di Prima, Allen Ginsberg, Gregory Corso, Amiri Baraka, Ira Cohen and many other kindred spirits. He has published novels, short stories, poetry, and essays that have been translated into many languages, including Danish, English, French, German, Polish, and Spanish. Last year, Ekstasis Editions, in Victoria, British Columbia, published *Tantric Picnic: Tales of India*, the first English language collection of his India stories.

Mikel K Poet is a poet and a memoirist. He enjoys walking his dogs (mostly),and trying to figure out his cats (all the time). You can buy his book *The Delivery Guy* at http://stores.lulu.com/mikelkpoet. "I found Mikel K to be a refreshing and sometimes uncomfortably honest look into the life of a modern writer struggling to come to terms with a pre fabricated and often superficial, turn of the century, American society. The battle is dynamic and comes to an uplifting spiritually evolved conclusion. I found it a fascinating read!!!" —James Lewis.
Current poetry by Mikel K can be found in his Facebook Notes section. http://www.facebook.com/people/Mikel K Poet/1254733243

Robert Priest is the author of fifteen books of poetry, 3 plays, 2 novels, lots of musical CDS, one hit song and many columns for Now Magazine. His words have been debated in the legislature, posted in the transit system, quoted in the Farmer's Almanac, and sung on Sesame Street. In recent years his stint as Dr. Poetry on the CBC and his poetry videos on Youtube and myspace have helped him find a whole new audience. His most recent book, Reading the Bible Backwards was recently charted at number two on the Globe and Mail's poetry list. (ECW) *Reading the Bible Backwards* can be securely purchased online at:
http://www.ecwpress.com/books/reading_bible_backwards.
Websites of interest: www.youtube/greatbigfaced (wherein the author appears naked with horses); www.doctorpoetry.com (a site where the author's avatar can be prompted to speak aphorisms); poempainter.com (the author's official website). Robert Priest also tweets as Doctor Poetry at http://twitter.com/doctorpoetry

Deena Remiel is an author of contemporary paranormal romance and poetry. She teaches language arts to middle school students. Curiously, she finds herself writing all sorts of correspondence for family and friends. Remiel belongs to RWA national and the Desert Rose Chapter of RWA. Remiel grew up in Philadelphia, home of the most amazing soft pretzels, and the Liberty Bell. School was her favorite thing to do besides using her imagination in play, and then in writing. After graduating from Hofstra University, and getting her teaching certification at Rider University, she became a teacher, and has been for twenty years. She and her husband began their own family in New Jersey until Arizona called her spirit to much better weather. Come for a visit at my website at www.deenaremiel.com

John Roche is an Associate Professor of English at Rochester Institute of Technology, where he advises the campus literary magazine, *Signatures*, and teaches a variety of literature and creative writing classes. He earned an MA from University College Dublin, and a PhD from SUNY Buffalo, where he studied with Robert Creeley and John C. Clarke. His full length poetry collections, *Topicalities* (2008) and *On Conesus* (2005) are available from Foothills Publishing (Kanona, NY). His poems have appeared in magazines like *Yellow Medicine Review, Flurb, House Organ, Big Bridge, Jack Magazine, Interim, Intent, Coe Review, The Woodstock Journal, Buff, The Burning World*, and in several anthologies. He also edited the collection *Uncensored Songs* for Sam Abrams (Spuyten Duyvil, 2008), featuring poems by Amiri Baraka, Ed Sanders, Bob Holman, Anne Waldman, Andrei Codrescu, and other friends of an emeritus RIT professor. Dr. Roche sits on the Board of BOA Editions, one of the nation's leading non-profit poetry presses. He co-edited with Patricia Roth Schwartz, an anthology of poetry by inmates at Auburn Prison called *Doing Time to Cleanse My Mind* (FootHills Publishing, 2009). A new book of poems, *Road Ghosts*, will appear in January 2011, simultaneously online at Bigbridge.org and in print from theenk Books (Palmyra, NY).

David A. Ross was born January 6, 1953 in Chicago, Illinois. In addition to his career as a novelist (*Good Morning Corfu*, 2009, Open Books; *How High The Wall*, 2008, Open Books; *Sacrifice and the Sweet Life*, 2003, Escape Media; *A Winter Garden*, 2003, Escape Media; *Stones*, 2001, Escape Media; *Xenos*, 1998, Escape Media; *The Trouble With Paradise*, 1997, Escape Media), he is a former columnist and contributing editor for *Southwest Art Magazine* (1984 1985). His first novel, *The Trouble With Paradise*, was awarded third prize in the 1997 National Writer's Association Novel Competition. David A. Ross lives on the Island of Corfu, Greece, where he is the editor of Moronic Ox Literary & Cultural Journal and Corfu Magazine.

Michael Rothenberg is editor and publisher of *Big Bridge*, www.bigbridge.org. His poetry books include *The Paris Journals* (Fish Drum Press), *Unhurried Vision* (La Alameda/University of New Mexico Press), *Choose* (Big Bridge Press) and *My Youth As A Train* (Foothills Publishing, 2010). He is also author of the eco-spy thriller *Punk Rockwell*. Rothenberg has edited the selected works of Philip Whalen, Joanne Kyger, David Meltzer and Ed Dorn for Penguin Poet Series and *The Collected Poems of Philip Whalen* for Wesleyan University Press.

Ernest Stewart, a.k.a. Uncle Ernie, is an unabashed radical, author, stand up comic, DJ, actor, political pundit and for the last 9 years publisher of *Issues & Alibis Magazine*. He is an actor, writer and a producer for "W the Movie." His lit site is at: http://uncle ernie.com. The magazine is at: http://www.issuesandalibis.org

Harris Schiff is a post capitalist utopian poet currently living in Park Slope, Brooklyn where he is raising two sons, Logan and Jesse. Former East Village resident, he was associated with The St. Mark's Poetry Project in the 60s, 70s and 80s. His books include *In The Heart of the Empire* and *Yo Yo's With Money* (with Ted Berrigan). His email address is Cagebreak@aol.com.

Melissa Studdard's new children's book is entitled *Six Weeks to Yehidah* (August 2011, All Things That Matter Press). Studdard is a contributing editor for both Tiferet and The Criterion and a Reviewer at Large for The *National Poetry Review*. She hosts Tiferet Talk , Tiferet Journal's blogtalk radio program. Her work has appeared in numerous journals, including *Boulevard, Gradiva, Dash*, and *Chelsea*. She holds an MFA from Sarah Lawrence College and teaches English and Creative Writing for Lone Star College Tomball.

Diana May-Waldman is an award-winning journalist whose poetry has appeared in numerous journals. She is the Bureau Chief for, and writes for, Worldwide Hippies and thinks everyone should. Her poetry and essays have appeared in numerous other publications, including *Cosmopolitan Magazine* and *Woman's Day*. Diana also co-edited with her husband, Mitchell Waldman (author of the novel, *A Face in the Moon*), the anthology, *Wounds of War: Poets for Peace*. She is the author of the poetry collection, *A Woman's Song*, and is Poetry Editor for *Blue Lake Review*. Waldman is a strong women's and children's advocate. She grew up in Ohio and currently resides in Rochester, NY.

Mitchell Waldman's short story collection, *Petty Offenses and Crimes of the Heart*, was published by Wind Publications in August, 2011. He is also the author of the novel, *A Face in the Moon*. Waldman's short stories, poetry, and essays have appeared in many publications, including, among others, *Worldwide Hippies, The Fringe Magazine, Waterhouse Review, Wind Magazine, The Fine Line, The Legendary, The Houston Literary Review, The Greensilk Journal, Eunoia Review, The Big Stupid Review, red fez, Connotation Press, The Battered Suitcase, eFiction Magazine, Midwest Literary Magazine, Wilderness House Literary Review, Moronic Ox Literary and Cultural Journal, Poetpourri, Poetry Motel, The*

Advocate, Bold Print, Desperate Act, HazMat Review, Mobius, Innisfree, The Rochester Times Union, and the anthologies, *Beyond Lament: Poets of the World Bearing Witness to the Holocaust* (Northwestern University Press, 1998), *America Remembered* (Virgogray Press, 2010), Green (MLM, 2011), Looking Beyond (Scars Publications, 2011) and Prominent Pen (dirt edition) (Scars Publications, 2011). Waldman also co-edited (with Diana May-Waldman), *Wounds of War: Poets for Peace*. Waldman is also Fiction Editor for *Blue Lake Review*. He lives in Rochester, New York, with his wife, Diana May-Waldman. Check out http://mitchwaldman.homestead.com for more information.

Viola Weinberg. In 2000, Viola Weinberg was appointed the first Poet Laureate of Sacramento, CA. Winner of numerous awards, she has published five books of poetry was the 2008 Glenna Luschei Distinguished Poet. She resides in rural Sonoma County, California and writes in a yurt.

Brandon Wilson is an author and peace walker, who has spent decades walking historic trails from Tibet to the Middle East to Europe and the Alps. In 2006, he walked from France to Jerusalem with a message of tolerance, recreating the route of the Crusades to re-christen it as the Templar Trail, an international path of peace. The account of his journey was chronicled in *Along the Templar Trail*, a Lowell Thomas Gold Award-winner named 2009 Best Travel Book. For more information, visit www.pilgrimstales.com.

David Wiseman is a librarian by training, a cook by necessity, and an itinerant athlete by coincidence. He has met the devil a couple of times and come away from it with no more than a few bad habits and a prescription. He is fond of whiskey, hound dogs, and pork. Older than he looks, he has lived in the mountains of Virginia for 225 years. His work has appeared in *The Legendary, Clinch Mountain Review, Night Train, Floyd County Moonshine*, as well as other print and web-based publications.

www.ingramcontent.com/pod-product-compliance
Lightning Source LLC
Chambersburg PA
CBHW030310080526
44584CB00012B/518